WHAT IT'S LIKE TO BE A BIRD

WHAT IT'S LIKE TO BE A BIRD

ADAPTED FOR YOUNG READERS

From Flying to Nesting, Eating to Singing—
What Birds Are Doing, and Why

Written and Illustrated by
DAVID ALLEN SIBLEY

DELACORTE PRESS

Copyright © 2023 by David Allen Sibley

All rights reserved. Published in the United States by Delacorte Press, an imprint of Random House Children's Books, a division of Penguin Random House LLC, New York.

This work is based on *What It's Like to Be a Bird,* copyright © 2020, by David Allen Sibley. Originally published in hardcover by Alfred A. Knopf, a division of Penguin Random House LLC, New York, in 2020.

Delacorte Press is a registered trademark and the colophon is a trademark of Penguin Random House LLC.

Visit us on the Web! rhcbooks.com

Educators and librarians, for a variety of teaching tools, visit us at RHTeachersLibrarians.com

Library of Congress Cataloging-in-Publication Data is available upon request.
ISBN 978-0-593-43018-7 (hardcover) — ISBN 978-0-593-43019-4 (lib. bdg.) — ISBN 978-0-593-43021-7 (ebook)

The text of this book is set in 10-point Whitney Book.
Interior design by Cathy Bobak and Tom Carling

MANUFACTURED IN CHINA
10 9 8 7 6 5 4 3 2 1
First Edition

Contents

Preface

For a long time, I planned to write and illustrate a bird guide for young readers. Having already written many books about birds, I wanted this one to be an introduction, focused less on the details of how to recognize and identify birds, and more on the fascinating things they do.

After years of researching and writing, my hope is that these pages will give you some sense of what it's like to be a bird and give you a deeper appreciation of these amazing creatures. It's a book that doesn't even have to be read in order—you can flip to any page. Most essays describe a single topic or bird, yet the book as a whole gets at something bigger and deeper: the ideas of nature and evolution, of instinct, and of survival.

Everything on our earth, you'll soon see, is interconnected: animals, plants, humans, and climate.

Birds have been around for millions of years, since dinosaurs roamed the earth. Throughout that time, birds have been constantly evolving: everything from their shapes and their feather patterns to their methods for attracting mates or camouflaging themselves from predators. But something surprised me when researching this book: A bird's life is far richer, more complex, and more "thoughtful" than I had imagined. And if that was news to me after a lifetime of watching birds, it must be surprising to other people as well.

Birds make decisions all the time, about what to eat, how to avoid bad weather, how to protect their young, and beyond. Much of this is instinctive—meaning it comes naturally to birds, like a set of instructions written in DNA and passed down through generations. Yet birds can balance many competing needs and adjust to different priorities and environments.

My growing sense as I worked on this book is that, through all these challenges, birds decide what they do.

For example, a one-year-old bird can build a complicated nest that looks and works like every other nest of its species, guided only by instinct. Amazing. But that same bird can also change its approach to building a nest, depending on its surroundings. It can choose different materials, add more layers to stay warm in cold weather, and more. And the choice of exactly where and when to build a nest is based on complex decision-making.

Or consider how wild birds face competing risks every day: starvation and predation. They must eat without being eaten. And they must find enough food every day to last through the long night. Finding food requires searching, often out in the open where predators roam. On top of that, eating adds weight, which can slow birds down, making it harder to escape. So they are constantly deciding between the pluses and minuses of any food source.

Birds are guided by instinct, but they are not simply obeying it like robots. Instinct must be more subtle, an urge or a feeling, not a command. The easiest way to compare this to our own experience is to imagine that birds are motivated by feelings: feelings of satisfaction, anxiety, pride, fear, etc. I realize this is very anthropomorphic, meaning it assigns what we think of as human behaviors to animals. But how else do we explain the complex decisions that birds make every day to survive? I'm not suggesting that birds talk to each other about feeling proud or satisfied or scared. I am suggesting that these same feelings in us humans could be the stirrings of instinct, too—to eat and live well, to thrive and survive, and to protect ourselves and others.

This book is about what it's like to be a bird, and that can perhaps best be explained in terms of how it compares to being human. In my researching and writing, I have been surprised many times to learn which things we share with birds, and just as surprised at other times to learn how different we are. I hope this book will inform and inspire you, the reader, to be a more curious and active observer of the natural world, and lead to a deeper understanding and appreciation of birds and our shared planet.

How to Use This Book

Range

This book is an introduction to the science of birds. It's not a complete guide, though. In fact, it barely scratches the surface of their world. That's because there are over ten thousand species of birds on earth and they do so many incredible things. The species of birds included here are a selection of the most common and/or familiar in the continental United States and Canada. Much of the science described here applies to birds anywhere in the world, though. Throughout this book are tips on observing birds closely and treating them and the environment well.

Organization

The book is designed to be read however you want. You can browse through it casually, out of order. Or you can read it straight through. Different topics may spark connections, perhaps even a sense of discovery.

Part I is the Introduction, an overview of birds. This section hints at all the rich comparisons there are to draw between different species. It will help you start thinking about the many exciting, diverse things there are to discover about birds. You'll also learn some key words and phrases that will come up throughout the text.

Part II is the heart of this book: the Portfolio of Birds. In this section, on the left-hand page, you'll find large paintings of birds that are *roughly life-size*. The right-hand page is devoted to short essays with fascinating facts and information about species and their habits, related species, and more. The section begins with geese and ends with blackbirds so that all waterbirds come before all land birds (with some exceptions).

Some topics, such as bird vision, come up in multiple essays throughout the book, each highlighting a different aspect of vision and how it varies among species. Some topics could apply to any species (for example, all birds have feathers and a similar respiratory system).

Bird Identification

There are so many kinds of birds. It can seem intimidating to recognize which is which or remember their names. Some may blur together at first, but they'll start to seem more distinct as you grow more familiar with them out in the world and through the pages of this book. One of the keys to identifying birds is observing differences and similarities. This will also give you clues about which species are related. Over time, different songs, sizes, and shapes will become more noticeable, too.

Consider, for example, the wide variety of bill shapes. As you watch birds' feeding habits, you will spot patterns in how each kind of bill (pointy, long, short, etc.) is used. Or how about all the different shapes and colors of wings? Color is one of the easiest clues to tell similar species apart. So are birds' habits. For example, the tilting flight of a Turkey Vulture is totally different from the undulating flight of most songbirds or from the smooth, graceful flight of a swallow. Wrens can often be identified by their habit of raising their tails, while phoebes have a habit of wagging their tails. There are countless more examples to discover, some of which are outlined in the pages ahead.

Disclaimer

This book is a very selective review of bird science. That means it's not complete! Instead, it covers the topics I found most intriguing during my research over the last few years. Many of the topics involve recent discoveries and thrilling possibilities still being studied, researched, and debated by experts. I have pointed out uncertainties and unknowns that are still, literally, up in the air. Writing such brief summaries requires simplification. Consider these essays an introduction.

Introduction

The Diversity of Birds

It's now common knowledge that birds descended from dinosaurs. But that doesn't make that fact any less shocking. Some dinosaurs grew feathers more than 160 million years ago, giving rise to true birds. Sixty-six million years ago, a meteor impact wiped out more than two-thirds of all terrestrial species in the Cretaceous-Paleogene Mass Extinction—including all dinosaurs and all but a few bird species. That's a shocking amount of time to compute, but it's true; birds really have been around and evolving for that long. Today, there are thought to be about eleven thousand species of birds on earth. About eight hundred of them live in the United States and Canada, and they are incredibly diverse. Their remarkable adaptations and abilities are presented in this book.

A feathered dinosaur known as *Anchiornis*

EVOLUTION—NATURAL SELECTION AND SEXUAL SELECTION

It has taken millions of years for birds to evolve and become so diverse. Charles Darwin's idea of "survival of the fittest" states that a species evolves over time based on "natural selection." In nature, threats like disease, weather, or predators remove the "less fit" individuals from the population. On the other hand, those who—living in the very same circumstances—have the characteristics that allow them to thrive are "selected" to survive.

At the same time, members of the opposite sex select mates who have appealing characteristics, for reasons ranging from their attractiveness to their ability to find food.

How are these two things related? They both affect which individual birds survive and reproduce—which then influences the characteristics that will appear in the next generation of birds. This leads to the wide range of bill shapes, wing shapes, nesting habits, and so on, because birds with the best adapted features are stronger and healthier, raise more young, and pass along their traits to more offspring. This process doesn't happen in a few months or even in a lifetime. It takes place over hundreds of millions of generations, and it leads to the diversity of life on earth.

Feathers

THE FUNCTION OF FEATHERS

What does a feather look like? Maybe you think of an oval shape or a long, straight shaft surrounded by soft, furlike strands known as barbs on each side (like the one shown below). But feathers can really differ in structure and size. What are feathers for? Feathers have adapted to serve many functions. They keep birds warm and dry, provide color and beauty, allow birds to fly, and more. Feathers are very light in weight and incredibly strong.

▶ Feathers did not evolve from scales. The precursors of feathers were bristle-like and hollow. Gradually they evolved to become the complex structures that feathers are today.

▶ The structure of feathers is no accident; they evolved based on the needs of birds to adapt to their environments.

▶ Feathers are hard to break. That's because fibers run from the base of the feather shaft to the tips of the barbs, keeping them strong.

- Feathers have many forms. Even on a single bird, there are different kinds of feathers for each part of the body.

Feathers as waterproofing

- Feathers are water-resistant. Their barbs are spaced precisely so that water won't flow through them or stick to the surface.
- Waterbirds have stiffer feathers than land birds. The barbs on their feathers are also closer together, which makes it even harder for water to trickle through them.
- Feathers wrap around the underbelly of a swimming bird to create a waterproof shell.
- Owls' feathers are less water-repellent than other birds', which may be why so many owls roost (meaning rest) and seek shelter under cover, for example in hollow trees, away from water and rain.

Feathers as insulation

- Duck and goose down (which is what many coats and blankets are stuffed with) is the warmest, most efficient insulation known to humans.
- Feathers insulate birds from heat as well as from cold.

Feathers for flight

- Each part of the body has specialized feathers. The large feathers of a bird's wings and tail form a broad, flat surface that makes flying possible.
- Wing feathers have just the right combination of strength and flexibility to allow flight.

Feathers as decoration

Feathers have evolved many colors and patterns.

- Clusters of feathers sometimes appear to be hard, solid shapes. For example, the triangle-shaped crest on a cardinal's head or the "ears" or "horns" of some owls, which are really just tufts of feathers.

- Among the amazing variety of feather shapes and colors, some don't even look like feathers.

HOW MANY FEATHERS DOES A BIRD HAVE?

The number of feathers a bird has depends partly on the bird's size, and also on how much it needs waterproofing.

A House Sparrow in flight

- Small songbirds generally have about two thousand feathers, fewer in summer and more in winter. Larger birds, like crows, mostly have larger feathers, not more feathers.
- Waterbirds have more feathers than land birds, especially on the parts of the body frequently in contact with water.
- A swan's long neck is covered with a dense coat of feathers, with more than twenty thousand on the neck alone.

FEATHER MAINTENANCE

Feathers are critical to a bird's survival, so birds spend a lot of time caring for them. Preening is the most important way that birds look after their feathers. When preening, birds use their bills to clean the feathers on their bodies, and their claws to clean the feathers on their heads. Preening combs the feathers into place, cleans out any dirt or debris, and removes parasites, like feather lice. It also allows birds to spread protective oil (which birds actually produce themselves, sort of the way our skin produces its own oil) on their feathers to keep them healthy.

▶ Birds of all species spend at least 10 percent of each day preening their feathers, using a similar routine. Preening is so important that some details of bill shape have evolved specifically for this activity.
▶ A bird can't preen its own head with its bill, so it must use its feet. Some species get around this by preening one another.
▶ Birds bathe frequently, most likely because water helps to rejuvenate their feathers.
▶ A group of related aquatic birds called cormorants often spread their wings when they are on land. This probably helps dry the feathers after swimming, but scientists aren't completely sure.

GROWING NEW FEATHERS

Feathers wear out and have to be replaced regularly. Generally, this happens once a year. The process is called molting. But birds need feathers for survival—so what happens when they shed them? Most birds have evolved a very orderly process to molt slowly. This way, they can lose and replace just a few feathers at a time—without losing the ability to fly or to keep warm and dry.

▶ Feathers grow from follicles in the skin, rolled up around the central shaft. As the feather forms inside the follicle, it emerges and unrolls. The tip emerges first, with the rest of the feather following over many days.
▶ Humans have hormones that influence their body changes—during puberty, for example. So do birds! A single feather follicle can grow feathers with totally different colors and patterns at different times, triggered by hormones. Many species molt twice a year, and take advantage of feather replacement to change their color. During one molt,

they grow a drabber plumage in the fall-winter. During the second molt, they grow a bright plumage (to impress mates) for the spring-summer breeding season.
▶ A new feather grows only a few millimeters a day. Even small birds take at least six weeks to complete a molt. Large birds can take much longer.

A male American Goldfinch in summer plumage (left) and in winter plumage (right)

▶ Growing new feathers requires a lot of energy—and also makes flying and keeping warm more difficult than usual. For that reason, molting generally happens during a warm season and doesn't overlap with other demanding activities, like nesting or migrating.
▶ Geese and ducks molt all their flight feathers at the same time, becoming flightless for a few weeks in late summer. This puts the birds at high risk, but only for a short time.

Bird Coloration

Birds can look striking and colorful in very different ways. Their appearance is incredibly diverse. This is partly because birds rely on vision, so the way they look is an important signal to other birds.

▶ The color of each bird species has been influenced strongly by selection, for reasons ranging from camouflage to attractiveness and beyond.
▶ The color of a bird's feathers can be produced in two totally different ways: as a result of pigments or as a result of the microscopic physical structure of the feather.

Pigments

Pigments are molecules that interact with light energy electromagnetically. Certain wavelengths of light match the energy levels of electrons in the molecules and are absorbed, while other wavelengths are reflected. The color we see is the reflected light. There are two common pigment groups in birds. *Carotenoids* produce most red to yellow hues. *Melanins* produce colors ranging from black to gray to brown.

▶ Carotenoid compounds come only from a bird's diet, including fruit and seeds. Brighter carotenoid-based plumage color is sometimes thought to be a sign of health and fitness.

▶ Bright color involves more than just pigment. Many species have reflective white feathers under their bright yellow or red feathers. The white feathers act as a backlight that makes the color pop.

▶ Bright colors also pop when set off against black feathers colored with melanin.

▶ Much of what we see as green in birds is actually a combination of yellow (carotenoid) and gray (melanin) pigments.

▶ Besides being a pigment, melanin adds strength to a material. Dark wing tips are a common feature of many species. Wing tips are the part of the wing that faces the most wear and tear, but melanin keeps them strong. Melanin also creates dark spots on eggs, which strengthens the shell and helps prevent it from breaking easily.

▶ Melanin also helps protect feathers by resisting bacteria that attack feathers. This is especially important in more humid climates.

Structural colors

A much wider range of colors is produced structurally, without any pigments. Structural color is complex. Here's how it works: The spacing of microscopic layers or air bubbles inside the feather matches the wavelength of a certain color of light. That color is reflected strongly, while other wavelengths don't match up and those colors are reduced. The multicolored, rainbow-like sheen produced by a very thin layer of oil on water is an example of the basic principles: Oil and water have little or no color themselves, but the interaction of light waves with the thin film of oil produces a very colorful display.

▶ The brilliant jewel-like colors of hummingbirds are produced by the microscopic structure of the birds' feathers.

▶ There is no blue pigment in birds. The blue colors of the Eastern Bluebird and other species are produced by a structure that reflects blue light in all directions.

▶ There is no green pigment in North American birds. Bright green can be entirely structural, as in hummingbirds, or a combination of blue structural color and yellow pigment.

Color patterns

Birds' feathers have diverse color patterns, which have evolved to serve many different functions. Colorful patterns can attract members of the opposite sex. They can also be for camouflage, to blur the bird's appearance or silhouette.

▶ Patterns on individual feathers can be incredibly intricate.

▶ Individual feathers are only part of the picture. Altogether, a bird's whole coat of feathers can create a beautiful tapestry of colors.

▶ Flashes of bright color in an unexpected area can startle potential predators and can make potential prey reveal itself by moving.

A Northern Flicker taking off

Variation in Birds

Despite the wide range of variation in birds, the appearance of each age or sex within a species is generally similar. For example, adult males of any species all look like one another—but these males can look very different from females. Younger birds can look different from adults, and the same adult can look very different in summer and winter.

Differences between males and females

▶ In many birds, the male and the female look alike, but it is possible to distinguish them by behavior.
▶ In other species, the male and the female look very different.
▶ In most species, males and females are about the same size, with the males usually just slightly larger. In hawks, owls, and hummingbirds, females are significantly larger than males.

Variation with age and season

Coloration often differs between young birds and adults, but size does not change with age. Birds grow to full size around the time of their first flight. They remain that size their whole lives, whether they are one month old or ten years old, male or female. So if you see a smaller bird at your bird feeder, it is not a baby, it is a different species!

▶ In general, birds like to show off their brightest colors during the time of year they are looking for a mate—a process known as courting. Drabber colors are generally worn in the nonbreeding season and on young birds all year.
▶ Very young Northern Cardinals have dark bills and drab plumage—a contrast to the bright color they develop as adults.
▶ Young crows can be distinguished from adults by the color and quality of their wing and tail feathers.
▶ Some species molt to replace their feathers twice each year, dramatically changing their appearance at different seasons.
▶ In some species, males and females, adults and young, each have different migratory habits and will spend the winter season in different regions.

Regional variation and subspecies

Scientists classify birds as different species to help understand all the variation that results from millions of years of evolution. A species is a group of individuals that share a common ancestor and similar traits and do not interbreed with other species. But evolution is an ongoing process, and birds constantly adapt to new challenges and opportunities. When some part of a species' population shows differences from the rest of the species but still interbreeds, those populations are classified as subspecies.

▶ In many cases, regional variation is related to the way birds adapt to different climates.
▶ Bill shape evolves quickly in response to new feeding opportunities.
▶ Northern flickers from the western parts of the continent have red pigment on their wings and tail, while those from the eastern parts of the continent have yellow pigment.

Bird Senses

Birds experience the world largely through sight and sound, much as humans do. The vision, hearing, touch, and smell of many species surpass those of humans. Birds can also sense the earth's magnetic field.

SIGHT

Birds have excellent vision, surpassing that of humans in many ways. First of all, they can see an impressively wide range of wavelengths (including ultraviolet, which has short wavelengths and would appear below the blue band at the bottom edge of a rainbow). They can even see as much as 360 degrees at once in peripheral vision all around them, with multiple points of focus—totally different from our vision. Some birds can see clearly underwater, while others have excellent night vision or color vision. But visual ability varies greatly among species. For example, many birds actually see less detail than we humans do, but they make up for it by having a wider field of view and are better at tracking motion around them.

Color vision

▶ Eagles see about five times more detail than we do, and about sixteen times more color.
▶ Many birds can see ultraviolet wavelengths. Ultraviolet is present in sunlight and not visible to the human eye.

Night vision

▶ Birds with relatively large eyes tend to have better low-light vision in the dark, which also allows them to be more active earlier and later in the day.
▶ Owls are active at night and have excellent hearing, but they still rely mostly on their vision for hunting and socializing. Color vision is not helpful at night, so they see mainly in black-and-white.

Visual field

Human eyes focus straight ahead on a single, small point of detail. Birds' eyes, on the other hand, see multiple areas of detail. Most birds have very little binocular vision (where both eyes overlap and see the same image, like ours), and generally it is not very sharp. This means they have a limited

A Great Horned Owl

view of what's right in front of them. In exchange, though, they have a much wider view of their whole surroundings.

▶ Many birds can see a full 360 degrees around, and 180 degrees overhead, at the same time. Imagine taking in that much all at once!
▶ Eagles see four separate focal points, two on each side.
▶ Because their sharpest vision is to the side (rather than in front of them), birds need to tilt their heads sideways to look up or down with one eye.
▶ Owls' eyes are aimed forward, leaving a large blind spot at their back. This is one reason they need to turn their heads more than three-quarters of the way around.

Visual processing

▶ Birds process visual information and details more quickly than we do, which is critical for tracking fast-moving prey and for scanning their surroundings during fast flight.
▶ A newly discovered type of cone cell (the cells responsible for color vision) in the eyes of flycatchers is probably specialized for tracking fast motion. This is one of several adaptations that help these birds see and catch tiny flying insects in midair.

Underwater vision

▶ Some birds need to see in both water and air and have evolved flexible lenses to do so.
▶ Some birds hunt fish underwater at night or dive so deep that there is essentially no light. How do they find the fish? Nobody knows!

Other visual adaptations

▶ Can you picture the way birds—including chickens and pigeons—bob their heads when they walk? They do this to stabilize their view of their surroundings.
▶ Birds have a remarkable ability to hold their head perfectly still in space, while the rest of their body

moves, to keep their vision fixed on a target.

▶ Birds have a nictitating membrane—an extra eyelid—that protects the eye from damage and dust.

HEARING

Birds' ears are small openings on the sides of their heads, below and behind the eyes. Their ears are usually covered by feathers and surrounded by clusters of even more specialized feathers that help channel sound. Birds' hearing varies a lot in different species. Generally, their hearing is better than ours in sensitivity and processing.

▶ Birds' brains process sound more than twice as fast as we do, so they hear much greater detail; in general, however, humans hear a wider range of frequencies.

▶ Barn Owls can catch a mouse in total darkness, guided only by hearing; modifications of ear placement and structure allow them to pinpoint exactly where a sound is coming from.

▶ Birdcalls are loud. Their calls are very close to their own ears, but several adaptations prevent them from damaging their own hearing.

▶ When you're in a fast car on the highway with the windows down, the wind can sound really loud. So wouldn't birds hear the wind when they're flying fast through the air? The streamlined ear covering that nearly all birds have likely helps them still hear their surroundings while they are flying.

TASTE

▶ Birds have taste buds inside their bill all the way out to near the very tip. We humans, on the other hand, have taste buds only on our tongues.

SMELL

▶ A few bird species, like the Turkey Vulture and the American Woodcock, hunt largely by smell.

▶ Many birds can smell well enough to distinguish their family from strangers, tell males from females, detect predators, find plants infested with insects they like to eat, and more.

▶ Pigeons and other species can use smell for navigation.

TOUCH

Many species have abundant nerve endings in the tip of the bill, making it very sensitive to touch. The Roseate Spoonbill and some other species hunt almost entirely by feel.

▶ The tip of a sandpiper's bill is able to sense things nearby before even touching them.

▶ Filoplumes—tiny, highly sensitive, hairlike feathers—grow at the base of every feather, allowing birds to feel the movements of their own individual feathers.

OTHER SENSES

▶ Birds have an excellent sense of balance. That's because they have two balance sensors: one in their inner ear (like us) and a second one in their pelvis!

▶ Balancing on one leg is easy for birds, thanks to that extra balance sensor and some adaptations of leg structure.

A White Ibis standing on one leg

▶ They can even balance on a tiny twig while they sleep!

- Birds can sense changes in air pressure and predict changes in the weather.
- By tracking the sun's movement, birds have an excellent sense of time.

BIRD BRAINS

Owls have a reputation for being smart. But other species of bird aren't necessarily "birdbrains"—they are quite intelligent. Ironically, owls are among the less intelligent birds.

- Most parrots are left-footed, the way some humans are left-handed. Performing tasks with only one side of the body is associated with better problem-solving ability.
- Birds can recognize individual humans.
- Crows are unusually clever and curious, and they even understand the concept of trading fairly.
- Crows can also solve puzzles, in some cases demonstrating an understanding equal to a five-year-old human.
- Some birds can remember thousands of hiding places and key things about each item stored.
- Groups of birds (like groups of humans) are better at problem-solving than a single bird alone.

SLEEP

- Birds can sleep with one eye open, resting one half of their brain at a time.
- Some birds spend the entire winter in the air and even sleep while flying!

Movement

FLIGHT

Birds have evolved many styles of flying, but all share some adaptations that make flight possible. Feathers are, of course, a key to flight. Over time, their bodies have also evolved to be lighter, which makes flying easier. Their weight has concentrated at their cores, in a compact, central mass. Even if humans had extremely large wings, we could not fly like birds; we are simply too heavy, and our proportions are all wrong.

- Instead of heavy jaws and teeth, birds have lightweight bills.
- Birds' muscles are concentrated at their cores, with lightweight tendons to control their extremities.
- Unlike humans, who give birth to fully formed babies, birds lay eggs. Eggs allow female birds to continue flying while their offspring develop in the nest.
- Even egg shape is apparently influenced by the limitations of flight.
- Species with larger wings relative to body mass (i.e., their weight and size) are more buoyant and fly with ease. Species with a smaller wing area require higher airspeed to stay aloft.
- Only hummingbirds can truly hover in the sky; kingfishers and other "hovering" birds require some wind to hold their position in the air.
- Adult birds don't seem to be afraid of heights.

SWIMMING

Birds that swim face many specific challenges. The first is just staying dry!

- When swimming along the surface, all birds paddle with their feet. Most have webbed feet, but some have lobed toes, meaning they have extra flaps along the sides of the toes.
- When swimming underwater, most birds use their feet to paddle, but a few species use their wings.
- Murres can dive to more than six hundred feet deep in the ocean—but how they survive, and how they find food there, is unknown.

RECORD HOLDERS

- The fastest animal in the world is the Peregrine Falcon, which flies at 242 miles per hour.

- The fastest runner among North American birds is probably the Wild Turkey, at about 25 miles per hour. The fastest-running bird in the world is the ostrich.
- Fastest wingbeats goes to the hummingbird. Some small species can flap their wings over seventy wingbeats per second.
- Gulls may be the most versatile birds: They are very good at flying, running, and swimming.

Physiology

SKELETAL AND MUSCULAR SYSTEMS

- Birds' skeletons have evolved for flight. Their bones have grown simpler and stiffer over time, but actually not lighter than those of mammals of the same size.
- Standing on one leg requires almost no effort, thanks to the way their bone structure has adapted and evolved.
- Most of what we call a bird's "leg" is actually the foot bones.
- Birds do not automatically grip their perch when they sleep; they simply balance their bodies.
- The tendons in a bird's toes can keep the toes tightly closed with very little effort.
- Adaptations of the bill and skull help woodpeckers avoid concussions.

CIRCULATORY SYSTEM

- Birds' hearts are quite large and have a very fast pulse. Small birds have a heart rate over ten times faster than the average human's.

Migration

Different bird species have different migration habits. Some birds live their entire lives within a few acres. Others migrate every year from one end of the earth to the other. We often say birds go south for the winter and north for the summer. Really, few birds have such a simple north-to-south migration. Each species has evolved a unique schedule and route that matches its physical abilities and meets its needs for food, water, and shelter. Over thousands of years, as our climate changes, the birds' behaviors and migration strategies evolve to match the new conditions.

- Not all birds migrate—in fact, only about 19 percent of species do, mostly to access better food sources.
- In some species, males, females, adults, and young each have different migratory habits and tend to winter in different regions.
- Most small songbirds migrate at night. Deciding which night to fly is a complex choice based on many factors.
- When migratory birds find themselves in an unfamiliar place at sunrise, they get information from local resident birds about where to find food and avoid predators.
- We humans can help migrating birds by growing native shrubs and trees and putting out food and water in feeders.

A Black-throated Green Warbler

- Many of the species we consider "our" nesting birds in the United States actually spend more than half the year in the tropics.

Extreme migrants

▶ An Arctic Tern can travel 60,000 miles in a year, flying all the way from the Arctic to the Antarctic and back again.
▶ Some Blackpoll Warblers migrate from Alaska to Brazil and back every year. That's more than 7,000 miles each way, including 2,500 miles nonstop over the ocean!

NAVIGATION

▶ Birds have some extraordinary senses that help them navigate—for example, they can navigate by the stars, by the magnetic field, by tracking the sun's movements and position, by ultra-low-frequency sounds, and even by using smell.

BIRDS AS TRANSPORTERS

▶ Nesting colonies of birds bring nutrients from a wide area and concentrate those near the nest.
▶ Birds transport seeds by eating fruit and either regurgitating (spitting their food back up) or defecating the seeds in areas far from where they were eaten, sometimes hundreds of miles away.
▶ Nature is truly an ecosystem! Salmon swimming upstream deliver nutrients from the ocean to the forest, and this fertilizes plants, which attract insects that birds then eat.

Food and Foraging

Thanks to both their high metabolisms and high body temperatures, birds need a lot of energy—and that means a lot of food. Most of their day is devoted to finding, catching, and processing food.

▶ Birds lose 10 percent of their body weight overnight, every night.
▶ If you "ate like a bird," you might eat more than twenty-five large pizzas each day.

▶ A single robin can eat about fourteen feet of earthworms in a day.

HANDLING FOOD

Birds have no teeth and no hands. So they have developed some clever tricks to handle their food.

▶ Since Birds don't have teeth for chewing, the "chewing" stage happens in their stomach.
▶ Birds can swallow very large food items; a heron can swallow a fish equal to more than 15 percent of its body weight.

Bills

Birds eat with their bills. The bill has evolved into many different shapes and forms, depending on the bird and its diet. Browsing through the species in this book will give you a sense of how diverse bill shapes can be.

▶ Most birds handle their food using only their bills, and swallow it whole.
▶ The bill is a lightweight framework of bone with a thin covering of keratin, the same kind of protein that makes up our hair, skin, and nails.
▶ Birds that need to crack hard seeds require stronger jaw muscles, which means they will have heavier bills.
▶ Herons and some other birds have pointy bills, but they do not spear their prey; they catch it between the tips of their bill.
▶ Flycatchers do not catch flying insects in their wide-open mouth, they snap them out of the air with the tips of their bill.
▶ Pelicans use their huge bill and expandable pouch to engulf fish.

Tongues

Tongues are very important to birds and have evolved many specialized forms.

- Many species use their tongues to manipulate food in their bills.
- The tongue of hummingbirds is adapted to capture a drop of liquid and carry it into the bill.
- Woodpeckers have a long, flexible, and barbed tongue to reach into crevices in trees and extract food.

FORAGING METHODS

Birds have evolved countless methods and strategies for foraging, meaning finding food in the wild. Most birds find food by sight, but touch, taste, smell, and hearing are also important for some species (see "Senses" above).

Tricks to help find food

- Quail, like chickens, scratch the ground with one foot to uncover food. Towhees and sparrows scratch with two feet.
- Egrets lure prey with bait and other tricks.
- Woodpeckers knock small holes into trees to reach insects inside.
- Some species use a long tail to sweep insects into view.

Adaptations to help catch food

- Some birds steal food from other birds. Some birds even eat other birds!
- Some hawks have evolved great agility in flight, as well as long legs—which allow them to turn quickly and grab small birds in the air.
- Hummingbirds and flowers have evolved together over time: Bill shapes match flower shapes, and some flowers have features that attract hummingbirds instead of insects.
- Flycatchers feed on insects captured in flight. Imagine trying to catch a tiny bug while flying at full speed! Flycatchers' vision has adapted to make this incredible feat possible.
- Many birds dive underwater for food; some ducks simply tip forward to reach food underwater.

DIGESTIVE SYSTEM

Once swallowed, food is stored in the crop. The crop is an organ near the beginning of the digestive tract. Next it moves through to the gizzard (stomach), where it is crushed and ground up. Then it moves on to the intestines, where nutrients and water are extracted. Waste products are concentrated into excretion.

- The gizzard is where powerful muscles crush and "chew" food. Many species will also swallow gravel and sand, which helps grind up their food into smaller pieces.
- Some birds can swallow whole clams, which are then crushed and digested in the gizzard. The hard clamshells can also act as grit to grind up other foods into small, digestible pieces.
- It's normal for birds to regurgitate their food. In some species, indigestible parts of their food are formed into a pellet and regurgitated—almost like the way cats cough up fur balls.

STORING FOOD

Most birds simply eat food as soon as they find it. Some put great effort into storing food for later, as squirrels do.

- A group of Acorn Woodpeckers can store thousands of acorns for later use.

A male Acorn Woodpecker

- Jays store food for use later in the winter and are careful to keep their hiding places secret.

- A single chickadee can store up to eighty thousand food items in a season—and can remember not only where each item is stored but also some key details about it.

DRINKING

- Birds can drink their body weight in water in a day, or they can get by with almost none.
- Birds excrete concentrated "urine" so they don't have to carry extra water, which would weigh them down and make flying more difficult.
- Birds in hot and dry climates have many strategies to conserve water.

Survival

BIRDS AND WEATHER

Birds live outdoors through all kinds of weather. They use plenty of tricks to survive, but severe weather can be a big challenge.

- Birds survive storms by stocking up on food and then sheltering.

Keeping warm

With small bodies and a high body temperature, birds in cold climates often struggle to keep warm. Feathers are essential.

- Down is the most effective insulation we know of.
- Birds grow more feathers in winter.
- During extreme cold, birds reduce their activity and stay in sheltered areas. Tucking in legs and bills also reduces heat loss (similar to the way we might hug ourselves when it's cold outside) .
- A swan's long, exposed neck is especially hard to keep warm, so it is covered with a remarkably dense coat of feathers.

- Birds in colder climates tend to have smaller bills and feet (the parts of their body without insulating feathers) to reduce exposure to the cold.

Keeping cool

Birds are well insulated, and—just like us—they heat up when they move around. Imagine wearing a down jacket all the time, even when you exercise! Birds have to be careful to avoid overheating.

- Nests are important for insulation, keeping the eggs and young from getting too hot or too cold.
- Birds don't sweat; they generally cool off by panting.
- The behavior of desert birds has evolved to avoid exerting themselves too much during the hottest part of the day.

AVOIDING PREDATORS

Birds are hunted by many predators. Their appearance and behavior have evolved over time to help protect them. Their main tactics for dealing with threats are: Don't attract attention; stay alert; and—as a last resort—create a distraction.

Be inconspicuous

Many birds rely on not being seen. Their coloration can be a good camouflage.

- Many species have complex patterns that blend in with their surroundings. Killdeer and other species have bold patterns that both camouflage and blur the outline of the body, making them harder to spot.
- Many species can hide their colorful plumage to avoid drawing attention to themselves.
- Many ground-nesting birds have camouflaged eggs and select a nest site that matches the colors of their eggs.
- Parent birds generally build their nests in places that are hard to see and keep a low profile when approaching or leaving the nest.

- When birds sleep or rest, they often choose a place that is hard for predators to reach.
- One hypothesis to explain why many small songbirds migrate at nighttime instead of when it's light is that they are avoiding predators.

Be alert

Predators usually try to surprise their prey to catch them. They will often target birds that seem slow or inattentive, or they will attack from above or behind. Birds give loud alarm calls to tell the predator it has been seen and to alert other birds nearby. They also use tricks to signal alertness, to show that they are strong and not to be messed with.

- Many birds have plumage markings that create the illusion of eyes—a false face—presumably to make a predator think it has been seen.
- Many birds literally sleep with one eye open.
- Birds in a flock rely on their flock mates to keep a close eye out for predators.

Create a distraction

When all else fails, a bird will try to confuse, harass, or startle a predator.

- Small birds often boldly and loudly gather around to harass, or "mob," a predator.
- Many birds protect their nests by pretending to be injured and luring predators away.
- Large flocks of birds can fly in confusing swirls, and though their movements can seem to be choreographed, they are really just reacting to other birds in the flock, like a "wave" in a stadium.
- Flashy color patterns, like the white rump of the Northern Flicker, may help to startle a potential predator in the midst of an attack.

Social Behavior

All birds have complex social lives. Some species are very social, traveling in flocks all year or nesting in colonies.

Other species are quite solitary and associate with their mate only during the nesting season.

COMPETITION AND COOPERATION

Birds often have to defend their food and territory against other birds. There are many advantages to living in large groups and cooperating with one another, though.

- For birds whose food is found in large amounts, but only in scattered patches, flocking in groups is an advantage.
- For waterbirds in areas where nest sites are limited (such as islands) and food is unpredictable (as in the ocean), nesting in colonies is the best strategy.
- Groups are better at problem-solving than individuals.
- Acorn woodpeckers store food in a way that requires the cooperative work of a small group of birds.
- Crows have a rich and complex social life and usually travel in groups that include parents and their offspring.
- In some species, birds preen each other.

Courtship

Courting is the process of seeking and attracting a mate. Most species of birds have a long, intricate courtship process, which allows them to show off both their sounds and appearance.

- Cranes are some of the most noticeably social birds. They impress their mates through dancing and other displays.
- When Red-tailed Hawks court, they show off their flying skills and exchange prey and nest materials.

Red-tailed Hawks

- The male Northern Cardinal shows off his bright red plumage and singing ability and presents the female with food to woo her.
- Northern Flickers fan their tails and sway back and forth in a "dance."
- A singing performance also often includes a visual display. Some birds will show off bright colors that are usually kept hidden.
- Most birds mate for life. Smaller species have a short life span, though—which means there is only a slight chance that both birds in a pair will survive long enough to nest together again the next year.

SOUNDS AND DISPLAYS

Birds sing to show off to potential mates and rivals and to claim their territory and boundaries.

- Birds change their singing to impress different audiences. For example, they perform one way for mates and another way for competitors.
- Many songbirds inherit a singing style, but they must first hear the song of their species to copy it. Most species of songbirds learn one or a few variations of songs when they are young and sing those for their entire lives without changing.
- The Carolina Wren knows up to fifty song phrases, and a male Marsh Wren or a single Northern Mockingbird might have more than two hundred songs in their repertoires.
- Birds produce sound with a vocal organ known as the syrinx, and they can sing two sounds simultaneously—one from each side of the syrinx.
- The pitches in some birdsongs are related mathematically, like a musical scale.
- Some birds sing at night, mainly to take advantage of the quiet to send their messages.
- Many birds sing in flight, both for the impressive display and to broadcast their song over a wide area.
- Sounds can be nonvocal. The wings of many species make a whistling sound in flight.

- Most woodpeckers use their bills to produce a rapid drumming on wood in place of song.

Family Life

The main activity in a bird's life is reproduction. The process takes many steps: finding a mate, finding a territory or a nesting site, preparing a nest, laying eggs, incubating those eggs, then feeding and protecting the young. Altogether, this can take as little as one month in smaller species, up to four to six months in many larger species, and over a year in a few species.

Territory

Most species defend a breeding territory that will provide them with food, water, and a place to nest comfortably. This is the bird's turf. They remain on it for the entire breeding season. Some species even stay on their territory all year, without migrating.

- Most migratory birds fly back to the same territory every summer, usually near where they were hatched.
- Some migratory species also return to the same winter territories every year.
- Birds defend their territory against intruders and will get aggressive if they have to.

NESTING

After birds have courted and found their territory, they get down to the work of raising young. They have evolved many strategies for it. In this book, you'll see the full nesting cycle of three species with three strategies: Mallard, Red-tailed Hawk, and American Robin.

Timing of nesting

In general, birds rear their chicks at a time of year when there is lots of food available, so they can give their young nutritious things to eat. For most songbirds, this is the spring and early summer, when insects are abundant.

- Waxwings time their nesting to coincide with fruit season in late summer.
- Most species of birds have a very brief nesting season. Others, like Mourning Doves, can nest almost year-round.
- A recent study of nest timing found that many species have shifted earlier as the climate has warmed.

Nest-building

Each bird species has its own style of building a nest, with different materials, construction, and shape. Some birds build extraordinary nests for their eggs, others build no nest at all, and others don't even raise their own young. All this is instinctive but adaptable to local conditions.

- Nest-building generally takes four to seven days for the Red-tailed Hawk and the American Robin, but up to fifty days for the Bushtit.
- Woodpeckers excavate, or dig, nesting holes inside trees.
- Nests are important for insulation to prevent the eggs and young from getting too hot or too cold. There is evidence that birds build thicker nests in colder locations.
- Some birds don't build a nest at all; they simply lay eggs in a furrow in the ground and have many adaptations to help them succeed.
- Species that nest on the ground on popular, sandy beaches have to coexist with humans, our dogs and vehicles, and other threats.

Nest defense

- Birds can be very aggressive in defense of their nest, even if at other times they are gentle and timid.
- One possible advantage of nesting in colonies, or groups, is that all nests are defended by an "army" of many birds.

Eggs

- A single egg can be up to 12 percent of the body weight of the female bird, and she might lay one egg a day for multiple days.

A female Chipping Sparrow with one fully formed egg

- Eggshells require a lot of calcium, which birds must get from their diet. Some birds even try to get calcium by eating paint chips from houses.
- DDT is a harmful, human-made insecticide that is still used in some countries around the world but is now banned in the US and Canada. Birds unintentionally ingested it when eating bugs that had been poisoned by the chemicals. One of the side effects of DDT was to reduce birds' ability to process calcium, leading to thin eggshells and no reproduction.
- Eggs of different species have characteristic shapes, colors, and patterns. Apparently, flight habits of different species can influence egg shapes.
- Some species lay only a single egg. Some usually lay two or three eggs, as in Red-tailed Hawks. Four eggs is a typical number for many songbirds. Some species, like ducks, lay ten or more eggs.
- Broken pieces of eggshell on the ground indicate that a predator has visited or there's been an accident; an empty eggshell neatly split in half indicates successful hatching.

Parental roles

The roles of males and females vary greatly among species. Overall, females do more parenting than males.

- Species in which males and females look alike generally share parenting duties equally.
- Birds that migrate tend to be sexually dimorphic, meaning the males and females look different and have different habits and roles. The females handle more of the nest-building and parenting.
- In hummingbirds, grouse, and most ducks, no pair bond is formed, and the male takes no part in nesting or raising the young.

▶ Crow parents often have helpers, usually one- or two-year-old offspring from the same parents.

Incubation

Incubation is when the parent bird sits on the eggs to warm them so the embryos begin to develop. Once development begins, the embryos are very sensitive to temperature, and the adults spend up to twenty-three hours a day incubating.

▶ In most species, the parents begin incubating after the last egg is laid. This way, all the eggs develop and hatch together (this is known as synchronous hatching).
▶ In some species, the parents begin incubating immediately after the first egg is laid. Chicks then hatch on different days, in the order that the eggs were laid (this is known as asynchronous hatching).
▶ Incubation times are generally longer in precocial birds and shorter in altricial birds.
▶ Incubation is the most dangerous time for birds. Because they have to stay in the same place all day, they can't move around as freely to avoid predators.

Chick development

▶ Precocial young hatch fully feathered with their eyes open. They instinctively know how to find their own food and avoid danger, though they do still depend on the parent for warmth and mentoring, especially in the first week or so.
▶ Altricial young, much like human babies, are born naked and helpless. They require care for many days. There are pros and cons to being precocial or altricial.
▶ Some young birds are between precocial and altricial—they hatch fully feathered and mobile but still depend on the parents for food.
▶ In species with asynchronous hatching, such as Red-tailed Hawks, the strongest (usually oldest) chick gets fed first. The others are fed only if there is enough food. There's a serious benefit to being the oldest sibling!

▶ Young loons often climb onto a parent's back to rest, which is warmer and safer than swimming.
▶ On short trips to feed their young, a parent bird carries back food in its bill. On longer trips, birds will store food in their crop (a digestive organ) and carry it back to the nest to regurgitate it for their young.

Fledging

The amount of time young birds spend in the nest before they fledge (the stage when they first leave the nest) varies among species. Precocial young leave the nest just hours after hatching, long before they can fly. At the other extreme, altricial young are completely dependent on the parents and stay in the nest for weeks, until they can fly.

▶ Though baby birds often leave the nest before they are fully able to fly, they generally do not need help, even if it looks like they do.
▶ Birds do not "learn" to fly, any more than humans "learn" to walk. They simply develop the feathers, muscles, and coordination necessary.

Birds and Humans

Birds and humans interact in many ways. Birds have an influence on human society. At the same time, birds' lives have been altered by the human population.

BIRDS AND HUMAN CULTURE

Birds are important symbols in folklore. Their feathers, habits, and songs have inspired writers, musicians, artists, and scientists for thousands of years.

▶ There are similarities between birdsongs and human music.
▶ The structure of feathers and other details of bird anatomy continue to intrigue scientists.
▶ Humans mark the changing seasons by the migrations and songs of birds.

THE BUSINESS OF BIRDS

The earliest humans hunted wild birds for food. Until around 1900, wild birds were sold for both food and fashion. Now we raise domesticated birds for food.

▶ In the 1800s, hunting was responsible for the extinction of several species, including the Passenger Pigeon.

▶ Birds were killed for fashion, their beautiful plumage used to make hats and coats. In 1900, activists took a stand. They created Audubon societies, national wildlife refuges, and new laws protecting wild birds.

▶ Only a few species of birds have been domesticated by humans.

▶ Domestic turkeys originated in Mexico, and some were brought back to the United States by European colonizers.

▶ The domestic chicken is the most numerous bird in North America.

▶ For hundreds of years, feathers were the preferred implement for writing.

▶ The pet trade is very harmful to birds. Birds like Parrots and Painted Buntings are first trapped in the wild, then sold as cage birds.

BIRDS AND THE HUMAN ENVIRONMENT

The human population has grown rapidly. That has a huge effect on the rest of the world, including birds! The more people there are, the more space we take up and develop. And the more space we take up, the more we usurp birds' natural habitat and transform it into human habitat. Some species of birds adapt and benefit from these changes, but most do not.

▶ Rock Pigeons have adapted to nesting on the ledges of buildings—instead of on cliffs in nature—and now thrive in cities worldwide.

▶ House Sparrows apparently adapted to human agriculture about ten thousand years ago and have continued a close relationship to humans.

▶ House Finches have adapted very well to suburban life and often nest on window ledges and other structures.

▶ As human noise changes the soundscape, birds are changing their sounds.

▶ In urban areas, more birds sing at night, likely to take advantage of the quiet.

▶ Sandy beaches are in high demand for human use, which leads to conflicts with the birds that have adapted to nest there.

▶ The increase in huge factory farms, especially the use of chemicals to destroy weeds and insects, has been bad for birds.

BIRD FEEDING

In most places, all it takes to attract birds to your yard is a little food. If you offer seeds or other quality food, birds will find it and appreciate it.

▶ Hummingbirds (and other species) can be attracted to sugar water.

▶ Birds generally prefer natural food over a bird feeder.

▶ Birds never depend on feeders. Feeders do not prevent them from migrating or from seeking food in the natural world.

Ecology and Bird Conservation

Ecology is the study of how living things interact with one another and with the environment that surrounds them. Everything is connected in nature. Birds are an amazing example of the way the natural world links creatures to one another—including humans.

▶ The nest holes created by woodpeckers provide nesting and roosting sites for dozens of other species.

▶ Salmon are critical to the survival of many birds, simply because they deliver nutrients upstream.

▶ Fruit has evolved to attract birds so that the birds disperse the seeds and grow more fruit. Similarly, flowers have evolved to attract hummingbirds for pollination to grow more flowers.

▶ Great Blue Herons benefit from the habitat that beavers create.

▶ Fear is a powerful ecological force. When predators scare and distract their prey, they actually create opportunities for those even lower in the food chain to escape and survive.

▶ Through colonialism and travel, humans have transported animals and plants across the globe for centuries, releasing them in different ecosystems. This can have devastating consequences. Some species thrive but have a negative effect on other species and are called "invasive."

▶ American Robins are native to North America but have benefited from such nonlocal invasive species as earthworms, bittersweet, and buckthorn.

Survival and Extinction

▶ The Canada Goose has gone from being a rare species needing protection in the early 1900s to being abundant and widespread today.

▶ The Wild Turkey was nearly extinct around 1900 and is now common again.

▶ In many ways, Barn Swallows have benefited from human civilization. Barns provide nesting sites, and the surrounding farm fields are ideal foraging areas. On the other hand, they may have trouble thriving if insect populations continue to decline.

▶ The American Kestrel is under threat—most likely because of the loss of its habitat and nesting sites.

▶ Chicken-like birds in the grouse and pheasant family are hunted around the world, and many species are now very rare. A few are extinct, including the Heath Hen of the northeastern United States.

▶ Several species of birds have gone extinct in North America in the last one hundred years; the last Passenger Pigeon died in 1914.

Threats to Bird Populations

The main threat facing most bird populations is habitat loss (see "Survival and Extinction," left), which happens when humans cut down forests and trees or build housing or roads where birds and other creatures had lived. Other major threats include house cats, window collisions, and pesticides (which poison insects and thus the birds that eat them). Climate change is another big one. A recent study found that the total number of birds in North America has dropped 25 percent in the last fifty years. That's a loss of one out of every four birds!

▶ We rarely find dead birds, and when we do, there is usually a human-related cause.

▶ Most songbirds don't survive their first year, and the ones that become adults have about a 50 percent chance of surviving each year after that.

▶ House cats are serious predators and are not native to North America. It is estimated that cats kill more than a billion birds a year in North America. Cats living in the wild are responsible for most of those bird deaths, but even well-fed pets kill hundreds of millions of birds every year. If you own a cat, keeping it indoors is one of the best things you can do for birds. An indoor cat won't kill birds.

WINDOW COLLISIONS

Window collisions are one of the most serious human-related causes of death in birds, estimated to kill hundreds of millions of birds every year in the United States alone. The basic issue is that birds think they can fly into the open sky and trees that they see reflected in the glass. It may sound like a cartoon, but this happens frequently and is truly dangerous for birds! Hitting a solid pane of glass at full speed is often fatal.

CHEMICALS

Birds depend on having a clean environment. They also require healthy populations of insects, fish, and other

ACTIVITY

To prevent a bird from accidentally colliding into your window, help the bird understand that it can't fly through the window. Decals of falcon silhouettes are popular but not especially effective, since they leave too much of the window clear, and birds try to fly around them. One of the simplest and best solutions is to hang strings or place vertical strips of tape a few inches apart on the outside of the window. This creates a visual barrier with gaps too small for a bird to fly through but doesn't interfere much with your view from inside the house. You can even make your own strips with scissors and hang them up with tape.

food sources. Species affected by the chemical DDT in the 1960s have mostly recovered since its ban in the United States. But use of other pesticides has increased since then, and some of the newer chemicals are also known to cause harm to insect-eating birds.

▶ The Bald Eagle, now recovering, was one of many species devastated by DDT. Lead poisoning, caused by human products (like lead bullets, fishing weights, or house paint), is also a dangerous and serious threat to many species.

CLIMATE

Climate change due to greenhouse gases will seriously affect bird populations in the future. It already disrupts birds' migration and their natural cycles. Rising sea levels are a serious threat to coastal birds.

▶ The annual cycles of plants and insects are changing with climate change; some birds are adjusting, and others are not.
▶ If projections for future climate in the desert Southwest are accurate, many birds will find it impossible to survive there.
▶ Any changes we make to slow climate change will benefit not only ourselves but also all birds and living creatures.

WHAT IT'S LIKE TO BE A BIRD

CANADA GOOSE

A Canada Goose with its young

Fifty years ago this species was an icon of the wilderness. After a huge population increase, many people now consider it a suburban pest.

With its white chin and booming honk, the Canada Goose is a familiar sight and sound on ponds and fields across North America. A few decades ago, seeing geese in the spring and fall was a rare, exciting event. In the early 1900s, their numbers had been so reduced by hunting that none were nesting in the eastern United States. Over the last half century, however, their numbers have increased so much that they are now even considered a pest in many areas.

A baby Canada Goose, just a few days old

Geese—like ducks, sandpipers, and chickens—have *precocial* young. They hatch with eyes open, fully feathered, capable of walking, swimming, and feeding within a few hours. (Songbirds, in contrast, have *altricial* young, hatched naked and helpless with eyes closed, requiring two weeks or more of constant care and feeding to survive). Most of a goose's behavior is instinctive. That means geese hatched in a mechanical incubator, with no parents, can still care for themselves and grow into healthy adults. The adult goose in the wild protects its young from predators and other dangers, but it does not feed them.

Young geese form attachments to, or imprint on, the first plausible parent they see. Newly hatched geese can imprint on other species, including a human, or even on an inanimate object like a toy train!

A family of Canada Geese

Male and female geese look alike, which is typical of species in which both sexes share the work of caring for their nest and young. The male is called a gander, and the female is a goose. Unlike most birds, family groups of geese stay together throughout the fall and winter.

A Canada Goose pair—male on left, female on right

SNOW GOOSE

Geese often change the timing and direction of their migration in response to weather and food.

Snow Geese

■ The Snow Goose migrates long distances. It nests in the high Arctic and winters in huge numbers in the southern United States. True migration involves a whole population of birds moving for the season. They do this to take advantage of resources—such as food and comfortable weather—elsewhere for part of the year. In some species, migration happens on a strict schedule. The migration of geese is more loosely controlled by instinct. Geese can move throughout the year. They might cover long distances nonstop, pause, or even reverse direction to take advantage of feeding opportunities. Plentiful food and mild weather will allow them to stay north, while dwindling food supplies, a snowstorm, or severe cold will send them south. Along with a warming climate, this has allowed many geese to shift their primary wintering areas farther north in just a few decades.

■ Have you ever noticed that birds fly in a V? The V formation allows them to communicate—after all, they can see one another. Birds in a V also save energy by flying through rising air currents left by the bird in front of them. (The bird at the front of the V is working really hard, since there are no rising air currents in front of it to benefit from.) Each flying bird leaves behind a "wake" of swirling air. Air flowing across the curved shape of the wing creates higher pressure below the wing and lower pressure above. This difference in pressure keeps the bird aloft. Most of the wing pushes air down—a downwash. But the high pressure below the wing spills off the wing tip and creates an upwash there. Trailing birds shift to the side to avoid the downwash, and adjust their position so that one wing passes through the upwash left by the bird ahead. They even adjust their wingbeat rhythm and their distance to follow the same path through the air and remain in the upwash from the leading bird's wingbeats. To accomplish this, they must have a remarkable sensitivity to air movement, lift, and drag.

Molting Snow Geese

■ Feathers wear out. All birds replace their feathers in a process called *molting*. Unlike most birds, which molt their large wing feathers gradually and keep their ability to fly, geese and ducks drop all their wing feathers at once and grow a complete new set. During this time, they can't fly for about forty days in late summer. To molt safely, they find a secluded wetland with few predators—after all, without the possibility of flying, it is necessary to lay low and avoid danger. After growing new wing feathers, the geese begin their southward migration in the fall.

■ Birds have no teeth, and so they do not chew. They can use their bills to break up food a little, but most of the work of crushing food happens in the very muscular gizzard (the bird's stomach). Food is stored in the crop, a pouch at the front of the body, and then passes through the proventriculus into the gizzard. There, powerful muscles squeeze and grind the food. The gizzard is remarkably strong. For example, a Wild Turkey can crush whole walnuts in its gizzard, and the Surf Scoter can crush small clams. Snow Geese eat mostly plants, but they also swallow small rocks to provide a hard, grinding surface that will help pulverize the plants in the gizzard.

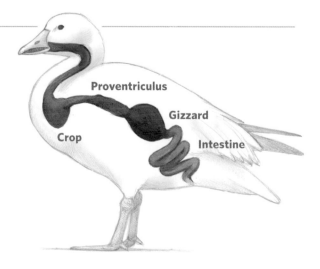

Proventriculus

Gizzard

Crop

Intestine

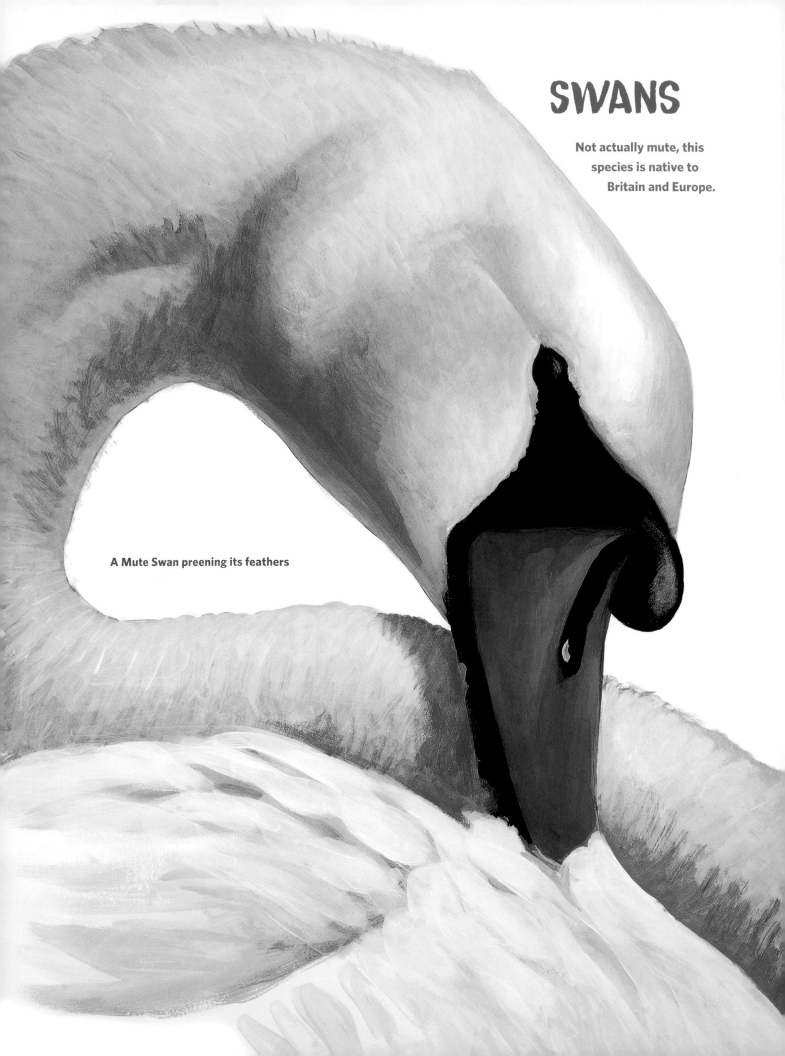

SWANS

Not actually mute, this species is native to Britain and Europe.

A Mute Swan preening its feathers

The aggressive display of a Mute Swan

■ Swans perform aggressive displays designed to make them look larger. The Mute Swan will lift its wings up above its back, fluff out the tiny feathers on its neck, and surge forward across the water—all while hissing. In most cases, birds are bluffing when they threaten a human like this, but the twenty-pound Mute Swan can deliver a powerful blow. Stay far away!

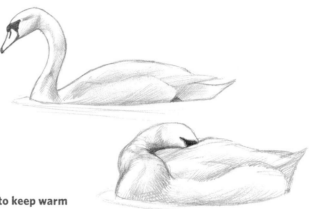

■ The long slender necks of swans and geese must be kept warm. These species will coil their necks tightly against the body when they can. They have also evolved a dense coat of tiny downy feathers over their entire neck. In fact, a Tundra Swan holds the record for the most feathers ever counted on an individual bird—just over twenty-five thousand in all, with 80 percent of those (about twenty thousand feathers) on the head and neck.

A Mute Swan curling its neck to keep warm

■ With their all-white plumage, long necks, and graceful manner, swans have been admired for centuries. The Mute Swan is native to Britain and Europe, where it was associated with royalty and was kept in ponds on wealthy estates as early as the 1100s. Beginning in the mid-1800s, some were brought to the United States and released in parks. They thrived and spread and are now common on sheltered waters from New England to the Great Lakes. Two species of swans, the Tundra Swan and the Trumpeter Swan, are native to North America. Biologists are concerned about the effect the non-native Mute Swan is having on native waterfowl; they are extremely territorial, and once a pair settles on a pond, they will chase off many other species of ducks and geese. They also eat large amounts of aquatic vegetation and could potentially outcompete native species for food.

■ What is a bill? A bird's bill is a very lightweight structure held together by two types of bone. A core of spongy bone is encased in a thin shell of more solid bone. The combination makes the bill both strong and light. Covering the bones is a hard outer shell of keratin (like our fingernails). Because it is living tissue, the bill can change color, though gradually. The keratin layer is constantly growing to heal cuts and scratches and to maintain the shape of the bill. The top half of the bill is the upper mandible, while the bottom half is the lower mandible.

A Mute Swan's bill structure, with the bones in gray and the thin covering of keratin in orange and black

DOMESTIC DUCKS AND GEESE

These are just two examples of
the many different breeds of
domesticated ducks and geese.

**Domestic varieties of Muscovy Duck (top)
and Mallard (bottom)**

■ For more than a thousand years, from the 600s to the 1800s, feathers were what humans used to write. The tubular structure of a feather shaft worked perfectly as a pen. Simply cutting diagonally across the shaft of the feather created a delicate, pointy tip for writing, with a hollow tube to hold ink. Trimming the barbs from the sides of the feather allowed room for a comfortable grip. The large wing feathers of birds such as geese and crows were just the right size. In fact, the modern word "pen" comes from the Latin word *penna,* for "feather."

The large wing feathers of a Graylag Goose, trimmed to form a pen

■ What is the difference between birds that are wild and domesticated? Wild birds grow or live in the wild in nature. Domesticated birds have, over time, been bred and adapted to live alongside humans. Only a few species of birds have been domesticated by humans. Two ducks—the Mallard (domesticated in Southeast Asia) and the Muscovy Duck (domesticated in Central America)—are among the most important. Shown here are just two of the countless varieties and crosses of these species that can be seen in parks and farmyards around the world. Other domesticated species of birds include two geese from Europe and Asia, the Wild Turkey from Mexico, guinea fowl from Africa, the Rock Pigeon from Europe, and, of course, the chicken from Southeast Asia.

Body feather

Down feather

■ Along with using wing feathers for pens, humans have found uses for two other types of goose feathers: Body feathers are used to stuff pillows, while the fluffy down found close to the body is used to stuff winter jackets and sleeping bags. No other material, natural or synthetic, matches down's combination of warm, insulating properties, and light weight.

■ In past centuries, geese were among the most important domesticated birds. The Graylag Goose of Europe even provided security, because their vigilance and loud calls made them "watchdogs."

A domestic Graylag Goose

DABBLING DUCKS

To reach food underwater, the Mallard and some other ducks simply tip forward while swimming and stretch their neck straight down to reach for food. This technique is called "dabbling."

A male Mallard dabbling for food

A Mallard taking off from the water

■ Taking off from water presents special challenges, since the water doesn't provide a solid surface for launching. Most species need to run across the surface to reach takeoff speed. Dabbling ducks like the Mallard are unusual in being able to launch directly into the air from the water. They do this by using their wings to push against the surface of the water. Their first wing beat is in the water, not the air. Once clear of the water, with a few vigorous flaps in the air, they climb and accelerate to normal flying speed.

■ The Mallard is the most widespread and familiar wild duck in North America, found in flocks on ponds and marshes across the continent. It has been domesticated, and many domestic varieties are found in city parks and farmyards. Waterbirds like ducks have many adaptations for an aquatic lifestyle. One of their main challenges is getting to the food they want, since it is usually under the water. Several related species of ducks use dabbling. These "dabblers" simply tip forward while swimming and stretch their neck straight down underwater to reach their desired food. This only works when food is within reach and not moving, so these species forage in shallow water and feed mainly on plants.

■ What happens to a duck's wings when it is swimming? The wings fold against the sides of the body. Then the flank feathers (found along their sides) wrap around the wings. Feathers of the breast, belly, and flanks form a complete waterproof shell, like a boat, that holds the body and wings afloat. When the back feathers spread out over the folded wings, they also fit under the flank feathers. Altogether, this forms a waterproof seal to protect the entire body from the water.

The top image shows a duck's normal posture, with the wing hidden behind the flank and back feathers. In the middle image, the wing is exposed. The bottom image shows how the flank feathers wrap around both sides to form a complete waterproof shell.

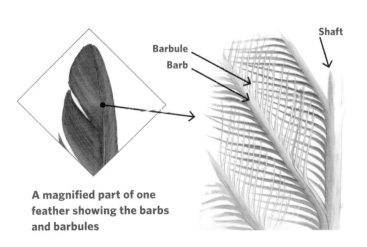

A magnified part of one feather showing the barbs and barbules

■ All birds have feathers, but no other living thing does. The typical feather has a single central shaft, with slanted barbs on either side. Each barb is lined with many tiny barbules. The barbules on one side of the barb have tiny hooks—known as barbicels—that latch on to grooved barbules extending back from the next barb. This sticks them together like Velcro. One reason feathers are so strong and hard to break is that fibers run continuously from the base of the feather along all the branches—right to the tips of the barbs and barbicels (the orange line shows a single fiber).

11

The nesting cycle of a Mallard

Two male Mallards display for a female.

The nesting cycle begins with courtship—the season when males vie for females' attention—which starts around November and continues through the winter. Once they pair up, the male and female will stay together through spring migration and during the stages of nest-building and egg-laying. The male departs once incubation begins.

The female builds a nest alone, on the ground, often under a small shrub or overgrown grass, and far away from water. She begins by creating a bowl-like shape, arranging dried grasses and other material around the edge to camouflage the nest. When egg-laying begins, the female still spends her time mostly with the male on a nearby pond or marsh and returns to the nest quickly and quietly only about once a day to lay an egg. During most of this time, the nest is unattended, and the female does little to defend it. After incubation begins, the female lines the nest with downy feathers plucked from her own breast and continues to add plant material and down to the nest throughout incubation.

Survival

A nesting attempt has only a 15 percent chance of fledging any young. Once hatched, fewer than half of all ducklings survive the first two weeks, and only about a third of those survive the next six weeks to fledging. Incubation is the most dangerous phase for the adult female because she spends almost all her time sitting on the eggs, relying on camouflage to avoid predators. In several studies, up to 30 percent of adult females did not survive the four weeks of incubation.

Once she lays all her eggs—on average, ten—the female begins to incubate, sitting on the eggs to warm them. She sits roughly twenty-three hours a day for about twenty-eight days, relying on camouflage, caution, and luck to avoid being seen. By now, the male's responsibilities are over. He travels, often hundreds of miles, to a food-rich wetland, where he will stay for the summer.

These young Mallards are about thirty days old, still weeks from flying. If they survive the threats of predators and other dangers, the ducklings will grow quickly. When they are about sixty days old, just two months, their wing feathers are fully developed and they can fly. Within a few months, they will look just like older ducks.

Soon after hatching, the precocial chicks are mostly self-sufficient—able to walk, swim, and find their own food—and the adult female leads them away from the nest. The ducklings still depend on her for warmth, though. She watches out for them and guides them away from danger. At this stage, the ducklings are extremely vulnerable, and many are taken by predators: foxes, cats, hawks, gulls, crows, predatory fish such as largemouth bass and pike, snapping turtles, and even bullfrogs.

When the embryos are triggered by the warmth of incubation, they will all begin to develop inside the eggs. So even though the eggs were laid over many days, they will all hatch together. About twenty-four hours before hatching, the young start peeping and clicking inside the eggs. A few hours after the first egg hatches, the entire family is ready to leave the nest together in search of good feeding areas.

WOOD DUCK

Why is the Wood Duck so beautiful?
Evolution!

A male Wood Duck

A female Wood Duck

■ Female Wood Ducks have a much drabber plumage than males, which allows them to camouflage themselves and avoid predators as they raise their young. In other words, their appearance has evolved to allow them and their offspring to survive—a classic example of Darwin's theory of natural selection. The adult female Wood Duck has an utterly different color pattern from the male, but she shares the same bill shape, a ring of bare skin around the eye, and a small crest.

■ One of the most beautiful birds, the male Wood Duck is the product of millions of years of evolution and female choice. The female manages the entire nesting and chick-rearing process alone. This means she can select a mate based only on his beauty—like flashy plumage and dance moves. Similarly to how dog breeders select their favorite dog characteristics, females can drive the evolution of these traits simply by selecting a mate. If she chooses a beautiful and desirable mate, it increases the chance that her offspring will be beautiful and desirable, and more likely to find mates themselves. This will boost the spread of their genes in future generations. Male offspring inherit the looks of their father, and female offspring inherit their mother's preferences.

■ The colors and patterns in bird feathers are mind-blowingly diverse and complex. Yet the pattern of each feather is extremely consistent across a species. How are these patterns so precise? Since a feather (like human and other mammal hair) is a dead structure once it emerges from the follicle, the only chance to create a pattern is as the feather grows. This is roughly like the way a sheet of paper comes out of a printer: Color is added to the feather before it emerges, beginning with the tip. Unlike the sheet of paper, which remains flat as it passes through the printer, the feather is rolled up around the shaft and fans out as it emerges. A single feather follicle can produce different patterns and shapes of feathers, switching between them based on hormones as the bird matures or the seasons change.

One flank feather of a male Wood Duck emerging from the tubular sheath and unfurling as it grows (top), and fully grown (bottom)

DIVING DUCKS

Scoters are diving ducks that find food in deep water.

Surf Scoters foraging for
clams in the ocean

■ Feathers are waterproof mainly because of their structure. The overlapping and linked barbs of feathers leave openings too small for water to flow through. The tiny hooked barbules not only keep the barbs from being pulled apart but also keep them all at the correct spacing. That spacing has evolved differently depending on a species' habits. Birds that dive underwater have barbs very close together to keep water from being forced through under pressure.

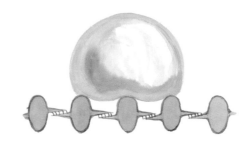

Like water off a duck's back—a drop of water resting on the barbs of a feather

■ Birds' bodies are well insulated, but they have no insulation on their legs and feet, which are often exposed to extreme cold. Birds' feet don't need much blood flow because they have very little muscle tissue. The bigger problem is that any blood that does go to the feet comes back into the body cold; however, birds use a system called countercurrent circulation to transfer heat and warm up the blood coming back into the body. The major veins and arteries in the legs split into multiple smaller blood vessels at the top of each leg, intertwining to allow more heat to transfer from the warm outgoing blood to the cold incoming blood. This system is so efficient that as much as 85 percent of the outgoing blood's heat is transferred to the incoming blood. Countercurrent heat exchange is widespread across the animal kingdom: birds also have it in their wings, and we humans have a rudimentary version of it in our arms.

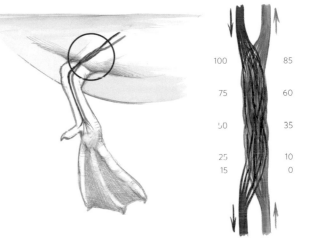

Outgoing blood in the artery (red) intertwines with incoming blood in the vein (blue); outgoing blood remains warmer than the incoming blood at every point (numbers indicate the percent of available heat), so heat is transferred through the entire length of the system.

■ In water birds like the Surf Scoter, each feather is very stiff and strongly curved so that its tip is pressed tightly against the feather behind it. Feathers grow close together and overlap to provide multiple layers of water resistance, all forming a firm but flexible shell that keeps water out and traps a layer of dry insulating down underneath. Land birds such as crows have fewer, straighter, more flexible feathers, forming a shell that is very water repellent but not good enough for swimming.

A cross section of the body, showing the feathers of a scoter (left) and a crow (right)

■ The Surf Scoter nests on freshwater lakes in the far north, and winters on open ocean. Unlike dabbling ducks, scoters are diving ducks that forage in deep water and dive to the bottom to find clams and other shellfish. Having no teeth, they simply swallow the clams whole. The powerful muscles of the gizzard pulverize the whole clam, including the shell, into pieces small enough to pass through the digestive tract. The shell fragments act as grit to help grind up other food. For this reason, scoters—unlike geese and other birds—do not need to swallow rocks to provide a grinding surface.

COOTS

Coots swim like ducks and are about the same size, but they are not related. The coot's sharp clucking and nasal whining sounds are very different from the quacks and whistles commonly heard from ducks.

An American Coot eating some aquatic plants

Most swimming birds have evolved webs between their toes, like ducks. The web creates a broad surface, which allows them to paddle efficiently, like the fins humans wear to go scuba diving. A few species, including coots, have evolved flaps along the sides of the toes instead of complete webbing. This makes the toes wider and provides more surface area to push against the water but still allows the toes to move independently, which might make walking easier. These are called "lobed toes."

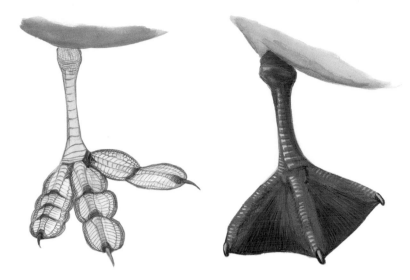

The lobed toes of a coot (left) and the webbed toes of a duck (right)

Birds have a well-developed sense of taste. They experience all the main tastes that humans do, although they have fewer taste buds. The coot shown here is tasting plants in its bill. Birds' taste buds are generally not on their tongues but in the roof and floor of their mouths. And they have at least a few taste buds close to the very tips of their bills, so they can decide if something is tasty as soon as they pick it up.

Green stippling shows the approximate position of taste buds (inside the bill).

Young coots hatch fully covered with downy feathers, with their eyes open, and can swim and follow their parents just six hours after hatching. However, unlike the fully precocial young of geese and ducks, they do not find their own food. Young coots are fed by the parents until they are several weeks old. This strategy is also shared by grebes and loons.

An American Coot offers food to its chick.

LOONS

The Common Loon is a beloved sight on pristine northern lakes.

An adult Common Loon with a chick riding on its back

■ Common Loons are known for their eerie, wailing cry and sleek feathers. Loons hunt by sight, so they live in clear, clean water they can easily see through. They rely on finding healthy populations of small fish, because adults consume about 20 percent of their body weight in fish every day. Acid rain, pollution, algae blooms, and silt from soil erosion can all make a lake unsuitable for nesting loons. Lead fishing weights that drop into the water can also be harmful to loons. If the birds swallow them, they get lead poisoning—which is the largest source of human-caused mortality in the species. For now, they seem able to overcome these challenges, and populations are stable or increasing.

■ Loons need wide open water to take off and can even become trapped if they land on a pond that is too small. They take a long running start, using their wings and legs to build up enough speed to become airborne. They prefer to take off into the wind, which helps increase the speed of air across the wings. Their legs are adapted for swimming and are set so far back on their body that walking is difficult, and taking off from land is impossible.

A Common Loon taking off

■ Loons forage for fish by diving completely underwater. Before they dive, they often put their head underwater to look for prey. Then they slide in headfirst. Using their feet to swim around, they try to get close enough to a fish to strike, grasping it (not spearing) with their dagger-shaped bill, and returning to the surface to swallow it. Loons can stay underwater for up to fifteen minutes and travel more than two hundred feet deep. On average, though, their dive is under forty-five seconds and within forty feet of the surface.

A Common Loon peering underwater and diving

A Common Loon with chicks on its back

■ Loon chicks often ride on their parents' backs in the water. Though they can swim within hours of hatching, they depend on their parents for food for almost three months. At three weeks old, they can follow fish underwater, but they rarely catch any; their fluffy down makes them too slow. At eight weeks, they have grown adultlike feathers and catch 50 percent of their own food. By twelve weeks they are independent, able to fly and to catch all their own food.

■ All birds molt to replace all their body feathers at least once each year. Loons and many other species molt twice a year, and loons transform from the striking black and white of breeding season to a plainer gray-brown and white in the winter. For the first year of their lives, young loons have drab gray-brown plumage that is very similar to winter adults.

A Common Loon in immature plumage

GREBES

Grebes may look similar to loons and other
waterbirds, but recent DNA research shows
that their closest relatives are flamingos!

Eared Grebe in breeding plumage

The American population of Eared Grebes spends most of the year not flying at all. Their migration habits are a multistep process. Each fall, they make a long, nonstop flight of hundreds of miles to either California's Mono Lake or Utah's Great Salt Lake (that's over a million birds at each lake). There, they feast on brine shrimp. Their entire focus shifts to digesting food, and their flight muscles shrink, leaving them unable to fly. When their body weight has doubled with stored fat, and food supplies in the lake dwindle, they stop eating. At this point, the digestive organs shrink to one-quarter their peak size and basically stop working altogether. Then

the grebes exercise their wings so that their flight muscles grow again, to prepare for one big flight. Their flight muscles must get strong enough while they still have enough stored fat to make the flight. They have enough fuel for only one attempt, since they are now unable to eat. Finally, in October, hundreds of thousands of birds take off together for their overnight nonstop flight over the desert back to the Pacific Ocean, where they will start eating again and spend the winter.

An Eared Grebe running to take off from the surface of the water

Amazingly, unhatched Eared Grebe chicks and incubating adults can communicate. In the last few days before the chicks hatch, faint peeping sounds can be heard from the eggs. The adults respond to these peeping sounds by turning the eggs more often, building up the nest mound, bringing food to the nest, and spending more time incubating. Once the chicks hatch, they ride on the backs of their parents for the first week. After about ten days, each adult grebe will take half the brood and the family will part ways.

An Eared Grebe tending its eggs

23

ALCIDS

Puffins are in the Alcid family, a group of birds adapted to life on the ocean.

An Atlantic Puffin feeding its chick in the nesting burrow

■ Alcids live in some of the coldest ocean water in the world, and spend the entire winter at sea without ever coming to land. They come to land only to nest in colonies on small islands or rocky sea cliffs. They are like the penguins of the Northern Hemisphere, though the two groups are not related. Their similarities are the result of convergent evolution. Separately, they each evolved similar solutions to the challenges of finding food in a frigid ocean.

A seabird colony on a small rocky island

■ Seabirds are essential to the ecology of their surroundings. For example, when a seabird catches a fish from the ocean and brings it onto land, that bird is also bringing the fish's nutrients onto land. These nutrients—which otherwise would have stayed in the ocean—fertilize the soil and increase plant growth, which then provides a home for many other animals. Another example: One study found that ammonia particles released from seabirds' excretion in the Arctic are an important component of cloud formation there, essentially helping to cool the region.

**An Atlantic Puffin,
from the front and the side**

■ The large, colorful bill of a puffin is a strange, wondrous thing and has earned it nicknames like "sea parrot." But why do puffins have it? The color is probably for show, a flashy pattern that looks good to other puffins. The shape and size of the bill is harder to explain. Most species with large bills, such as toucans, live in hot climates, where their bill actually helps radiate heat out of the body. But puffins live in very cold water, and such a large bill can make it harder to keep warm and difficult to move underwater. One possible advantage is that the extra height adds stiffness and keeps the bill from bending, allowing the puffin to clamp down tightly on multiple fish.

■ Murres, related to puffins, feed on small fish. They can dive to six hundred feet or more below the surface of the ocean—about a hundred swimming pools deep! At that depth, even on a bright sunny day in clear water, the light is as black as midnight. Are they able to see down there? It seems unlikely, but nobody knows what senses they are using. Similarly, no one knows how the birds withstand the pressure at those depths, or how they can travel that far and fast without breathing.

**A Thick-billed Murre
diving into the darkness**

My vision is blurry underwater—how do birds see and catch fish?

To focus an image on the retina, our eye relies on refraction—the bending of light as it passes from a material of one density to another. In air, most of the refractive power of the eye comes from the curved surface of the cornea. That clear outside layer is where light passes from gas (air) to liquid (cornea). The lens makes only tiny adjustments to focus on near or far objects. In water, the cornea has almost no effect as light passes from liquid (water) to liquid (cornea). Our lens alone can't compensate to focus the image on our retina, so we see a blur. But waterbirds have evolved a much more flexible lens. To create a sharp image underwater, a group of tiny muscles squeezes the lens, forcing it to bulge out through the more rigid iris, which creates a strongly curved surface that can take over for the cornea underwater.

PELICANS

An adult Brown Pelican in a relaxed pose. Pelicans are among the heaviest flying birds in the world.

■ Two of the world's eight species of pelicans are found in North America: the Brown Pelican, in salt water along our coasts, and the American White Pelican, mainly in fresh water and in the West. Both are instantly recognizable by their very large size and pelican pouch. The American White Pelican is more than two thousand times as heavy as a hummingbird! That's equivalent to the difference between a human and a blue whale.

DDT (represented by orange dots) accumulating as it moves up the food chain from insects to fish to pelican

■ The Brown Pelican nearly became extinct in the 1950s and '60s, when the insecticide DDT was sprayed across the United States. DDT accumulates in the body fat of animals, where it can persist for years. Insects each carry a tiny amount, but fish that feed on those insects are continually adding pesticide to their bodies. When pelicans eat those fish, they, too, absorb the many pesticides. DDT interferes with the body's use of calcium, so contaminated birds produce eggs with shells that break very easily. Pelicans were literally breaking their own eggs when they tried to incubate, leading to zero reproduction and a declining population. Fortunately, the trend reversed within a few years after the ban of DDT in the United States in 1972, and the Brown Pelican is once again a common sight along our southern coasts.

How a pelican fishes with its pouch

Contrary to popular belief, a pelican's pouch is not used as a basket to carry fish but as a giant scoop to catch fish underwater.

Brown Pelicans fly above the water, looking for fish. When they spot a school, they plunge headfirst into the water.

When they plunge into the water with the bill open, the pouch stretches like a balloon, filling with up to three gallons of water—and, hopefully, many fish.

As soon as the pelican's head stops moving forward through the water, the upper mandible (upper part of a bird's beak) closes to trap any fish inside the pouch.

Resting on the water, the pelican slowly raises its head, allowing water to drain out, while fish stay in the pouch.

Finally, when all the water has drained, the pelican swallows any fish with a deft toss of the head.

■ *Kleptoparasitism* is a fancy term for a strategy of stealing food. Some species of seabirds, especially gulls and their relatives, specialize in this behavior. When they see a bird that has captured a meal, they simply try to steal it for themselves. Laughing Gulls often hang around foraging pelicans, even standing on a pelican's head, hoping to grab a few fish. The gulls are looking for fish that fall out as the pelican drains its pouch, but will also take any fish they can get out of the open pouch.

Brown Pelican and Laughing Gull

HERONS

A six-pound heron can swallow a one-pound fish. Imagine a one-hundred-pound person swallowing a seventeen-pound fish. Whole!

Great Blue Heron

■ Great Blue Herons are very patient hunters. When they see their prey, they lean forward and coil up their necks, carefully planning for one explosive strike. In a fraction of a second, they have grabbed the fish in their bills. Out of the water, they move the fish with a quick toss so they can swallow it—headfirst and whole. Smaller prey, like minnows, go down with no trouble. Larger prey can take up to a minute to travel the length of the neck, with a bulge visible all the way down. After a very large meal, the heron may sit for several minutes to let it "settle" before going back to hunting.

■ It may appear graceful from far away, but up close the large Great Blue Heron is a fearsome predator. Its dagger-like bill is usually aimed at fish, but frogs, crayfish, mice, and even small birds are on the menu if they come within striking range. At nearly four feet tall, it is the tallest bird that most people will see. They are often seen resting or standing patiently at the water's edge, just watching. If disturbed, the heron will fly up with a deep croak, beating its wings slowly and deeply, and curling its neck back onto its shoulders.

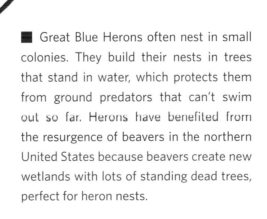

■ Great Blue Herons often nest in small colonies. They build their nests in trees that stand in water, which protects them from ground predators that can't swim out so far. Herons have benefited from the resurgence of beavers in the northern United States because beavers create new wetlands with lots of standing dead trees, perfect for heron nests.

Great Blue Herons at a nest

Great Blue Heron head-on

EGRETS

Egrets and herons have different names,
but they are all in the same family.

A Snowy Egret in
courtship display

Light reflecting off the fish (orange line) bends at the surface, so it reaches the egret's eye from a different angle; sighting along that line (dotted line), the fish appears to be in a different location.

■ Most egrets are white, and some species have lacy plumes. The egret's delicate feathers were the height of fashion in the late 1800s, and plume hunters killed hundreds of thousands of birds every year to make hats. By 1900, the populations of many species were dangerously low. Protests over the killing led to some great strides in animal activism: the formation of Audubon Societies, the first laws to protect wild birds, and the establishment of the US National Wildlife Refuge System. With protection, most species quickly recovered.

■ Herons and egrets have many tricks to get close to fish. Green Herons place small feathers (and even fish food pellets found in a public park) on the surface of the water and then watch for small fish that come to the bait. Snowy Egrets often vibrate the tips of their bills in the water to mimic an insect struggling on the surface, then catch any fish that come near. Bringing fish to the surface has another advantage: It mostly eliminates the challenge of refraction.

A Snowy Egret luring fish to the surface

ACTIVITY

Try dipping a pencil (or any other long, straight object) into some water. Do you see how the pencil looks like it bends at the water's surface? If you were targeting the very tip of the pencil, where would you aim? This is the egret's challenge, and it's known as refraction. Light reflecting off a fish bends at the water's surface (just as with the pencil), meaning the fish is not exactly where it appears to be. Yet the egret must try to strike the real fish—even if it's as much as three inches away from where it appears. Knowing where the real fish is requires a complex calculation of angle and depth. Experiments have shown that, before they strike, egrets position themselves so that the angle and depth fit a certain mathematical relationship, and this apparently allows them to correct for refraction.

The evolution of feathers

Though feathers developed in dinosaurs, they did not evolve from scales. The evolution of feathers is explained in five stages:

Stage 1: The earliest "feather" was a hollow tube, probably for insulation and protection. Even at this early stage, the feathers could have been colored for display or camouflage.

Stage 2: The simple tube divides into separate fibers from the base. This would create a layer of fuzz and more effective insulation than the bristly tubes of Stage 1.

Stage 3: A branch-like structure develops, with a central shaft and barbs along each side, similar to the feathers of modern birds. This allows more complex color patterns to form.

Stage 4: The feathers keep growing more "branches." Tiny barbules grow along each barb, with hooks that interlock like Velcro. Now the barbs stick together, creating a more rigid, flat surface.

Stage 5: Different feather shapes and structures develop for different functions. Some of the most complex, specialized feathers are those involved in flight—like asymmetrical wing feathers, which improve a bird's aerodynamics. This suggests that flight is a more recent stage in the evolution of feathers and not their original function.

SPOONBILLS AND IBISES

Roseate Spoonbill

Found along the southeast coast, from Texas to Georgia, the Roseate Spoonbill's pink color and spoon-shaped bill make it instantly recognizable.

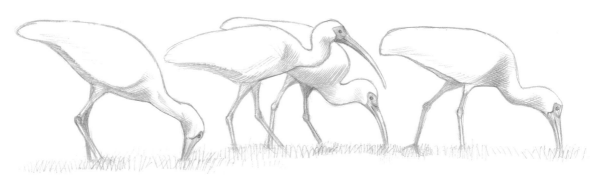

Feeding both by sight and by feel, White Ibises thrust their bills into mud or into burrows.

■ Finding food is one of the main challenges that birds face. Large wading birds—including herons, ibises, and spoonbills—use a wide range of strategies. Herons and egrets hunt only by sight. Ibises use both sight and touch. Spoonbills hunt only by touch. They feed by swinging their bills back and forth in muddy water, keeping them slightly open so water passes through between the upper and lower mandibles. Tiny prey, like shrimp or small fish, can be felt, grabbed, and swallowed.

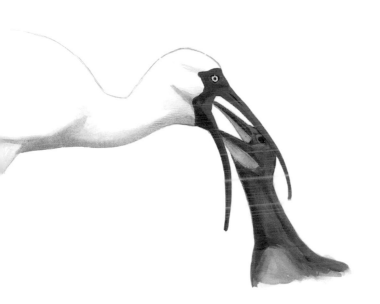

■ Regurgitation is normal and common in birds. All birds have a sac at the base of their neck, where the esophagus meets the body, known as the crop. It is mainly a food-storage organ. Adult birds can gather a lot of food while out foraging, hold it in their crops as they fly back to the nest, then regurgitate it for their young. Birds also regurgitate and get rid of indigestible parts of their food, like seeds or shells.

A baby White Ibis (right) reaches in for food being regurgitated by the adult (left).

■ Why do birds stand on one leg? The short answer is: Because it's easy for them! All birds do it. The center of mass of their body is below the knee, and they also have an extra balance sensor near their pelvis. Balancing on one leg requires angling that leg so that the foot is directly below the body. With the leg locked in position, and the body leaning against the leg, tiny adjustments of the toes are all that is needed to stay upright.

A White Ibis standing on one leg, from the side and from the front

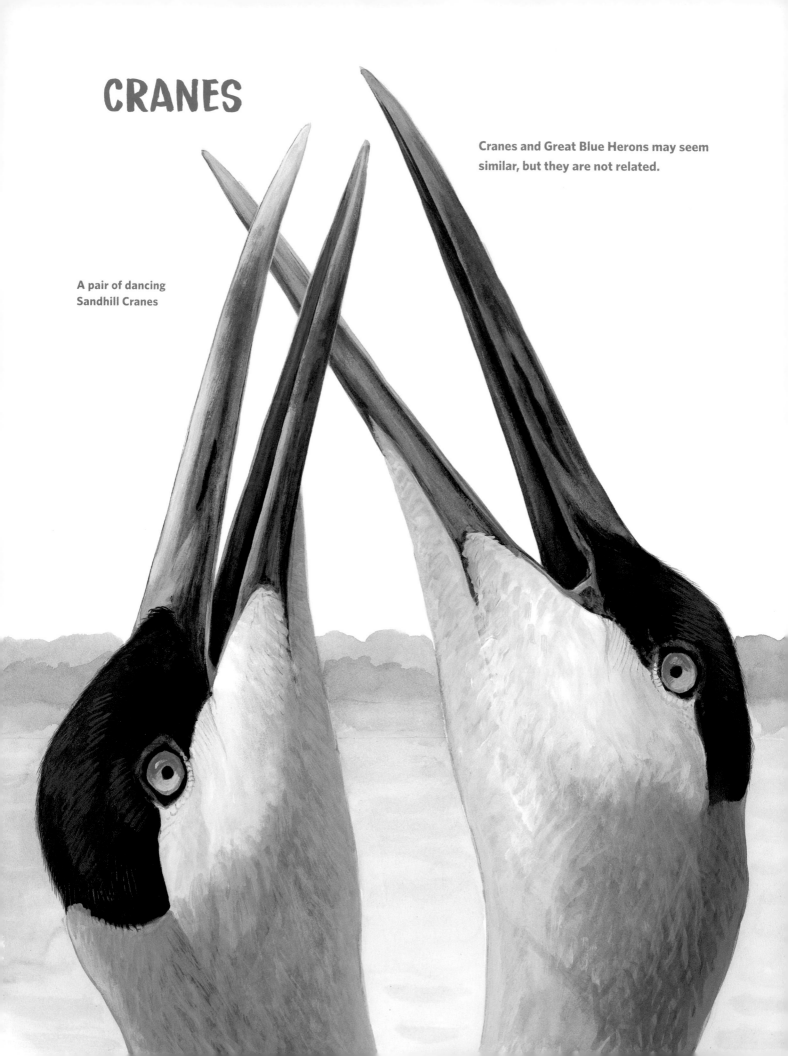

CRANES

Cranes and Great Blue Herons may seem similar, but they are not related.

A pair of dancing Sandhill Cranes

■ Cranes and Great Blue Herons can be distinguished by many details of appearance, habits, and voice. Cranes are almost always in pairs or flocks (not solitary) and have pleasing, bugling calls. While herons hunt fish with a violent lunge, cranes feed by picking food from the ground. Cranes also have a patch of red skin on their forehead.

Great Blue Heron (left) and Sandhill Crane (right)

The dance of the Sandhill Crane

■ At the end of summer, all cranes gather in flocks to migrate south for the winter. Within these flocks, they put on social displays, including the spectacular and intricate "dancing" unique to cranes. A dance is initiated by the male and involves bowing, calling, flapping, running, and leaping into the air. It is thought to be a courtship display, but it occurs throughout the winter, and dancing by one pair often stimulates other pairs nearby to join in and dance, too.

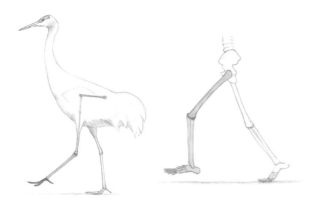

A human leg (right) compared to a Sandhill Crane leg (left), with toes, foot, lower leg, and upper leg each color coded

■ If you look carefully at a bird's legs, you'll see that the "knee" joint seems to bend the wrong way. That's because what you're looking at is actually the ankle joint. The bones equivalent to most of our foot (shown in yellow) are, in a bird, actually a long, straight structure that looks very leglike. So what we call a bird's foot is really just its toe bones. All the muscles that move these parts are close to the body, hidden and insulated by feathers, which is why the parts we see are so spindly and skeletal, really just slender bones and tendons with a leathery covering.

■ Most of the world's fifteen crane species are threatened or endangered. Only three of them have secure populations. One of those is the Sandhill Crane—whose population is, in fact, growing. The other species native to North America is the Whooping Crane. In 1941, there were only twenty individual Whooping Cranes alive. With the help of dedicated work by biologists, the population has slowly increased and now numbers several hundred birds in the wild.

PLOVERS

Ground-nesting birds like the Killdeer use camouflage and trickery to protect their eggs and young from predators.

A Killdeer nesting in a park

The first sign that a Killdeer lives nearby is the piercing *"kill-deer"* call repeated over and over from high in the air. This is the male advertising to rivals and his mate, claiming a territory.

Often, Killdeer nest on the ground at the edge of a parking lot, along a road, or even on a rooftop. But nesting on open ground leaves eggs and young vulnerable to predators. Adult birds have adapted to make sure their eggs remain undiscovered, and they have developed impressive tricks and strategies to keep them safe. Eggs may be different shades of camouflage, and there is evidence that the adults choose to nest on ground that matches their eggs. But visual camouflage doesn't stop skunks, foxes, or other predators from hunting by smell, especially at night. To protect against this, Killdeer and other ground-nesting birds have evolved to change their preen oil during the nesting season to a different chemical compound that has no odor. This masks the smell of incubating birds, making them less likely to be found.

The camouflaged eggs of a Killdeer, laid in a faint depression on open ground

A few species of small plovers live and nest on sandy beaches, just above the high tide line. There's the Piping Plover in the eastern United States and the Snowy Plover in the West. This puts them into direct competition with millions of humans who use the same sandy beaches for fun. There are only about twelve thousand Piping Plovers in the world. The survival of the species now depends on the help of some humans to educate other humans and keep them (and their dogs, vehicles, kites, and other threats) away from the nesting plovers. If the plovers are protected from disturbance at critical times, they can nest successfully even on a popular beach.

I saw a bird that was obviously injured, just flopping on the ground, but when I got close, it flew away.

This is all an act to protect their eggs or young, a behavior called a "broken-wing act," which is a kind of distraction display. The bird pretends to have a broken wing, calling pitifully, stumbling, dragging one wing on the ground. It can be very convincing, and as you follow it, you are being lured farther from the nest. When the bird feels it has brought you far enough away, it simply takes off and flies away. It will sneak back to the nest later.

A Killdeer performing a distraction display

Piping Plover

LARGE SANDPIPERS

A very large sandpiper with an impressively long bill, this species spends much of the year on dry prairie, eating grasshoppers and other insects they pluck from the grass.

Long-billed Curlew picking up a fiddler crab

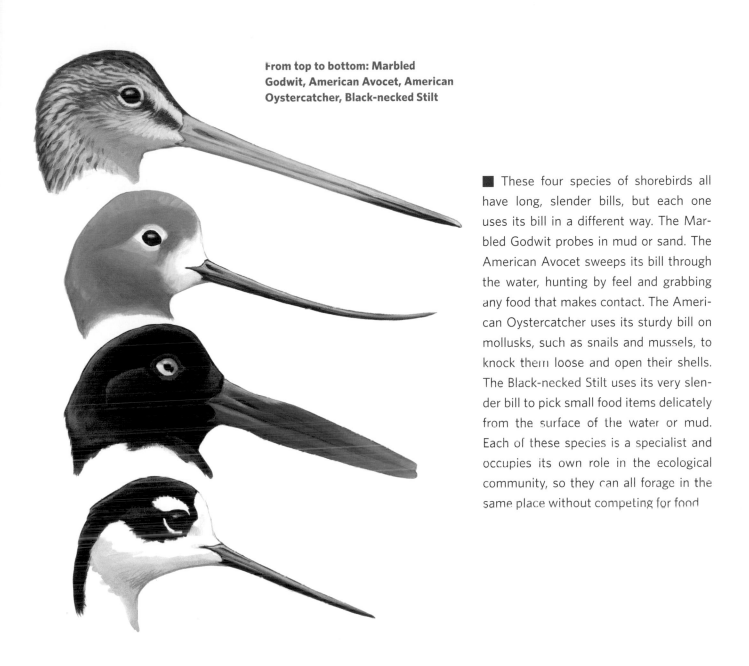

From top to bottom: **Marbled Godwit, American Avocet, American Oystercatcher, Black-necked Stilt**

■ These four species of shorebirds all have long, slender bills, but each one uses its bill in a different way. The Marbled Godwit probes in mud or sand. The American Avocet sweeps its bill through the water, hunting by feel and grabbing any food that makes contact. The American Oystercatcher uses its sturdy bill on mollusks, such as snails and mussels, to knock them loose and open their shells. The Black-necked Stilt uses its very slender bill to pick small food items delicately from the surface of the water or mud. Each of these species is a specialist and occupies its own role in the ecological community, so they can all forage in the same place without competing for food

■ The tips of sandpipers' bills are packed with nerve endings so they can sense their prey under the mud or sand, and they have taste buds inside the tips of their bills to test whatever they find.

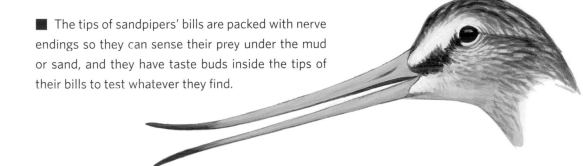

A Marbled Godwit flexing its bill tip to grab prey buried in the mud; compare the resting bill shape of the Marbled Godwit in the image above.

SMALL SANDPIPERS

Sanderlings running on the beach

This species spends all day running up and down beaches, looking for food uncovered by waves in the sand.

■ The swerving movements of a flock of sandpipers in flight are among the most amazing spectacles in nature. There is no leader—any bird in the flock can suggest a turn. The other birds see the change in direction and swiftly follow, much like a "wave" in a sports stadium. In fact, a flock the size of a football field can all change direction in less than three seconds. Each individual bird reacts and switches to the new direction. Being at the edge of the flock can give them a better view of any potential danger—but also makes them more vulnerable to attack. Some turns are in response to actual danger, but many are likely just prompted by a desire to get away from the edge. The result is a dizzying, swirling, unpredictable mass of birds that is very difficult for a predator to attack—which keeps the group safer.

A flock of sandpipers before and after a turn. The edge bird (light color) initiates the turn, all birds turn on the same radius in response, and the edge bird ends up in the middle of the flock after the turn.

A Dunlin probing in mud

■ The tip of a sandpiper's bill is extremely sensitive to touch. They can even sense things indirectly with it. For example, when the bill is in wet sand or mud, it displaces water around it. If the flow of water is blocked by something nearby (like a small clam), slightly higher pressure builds up in the water between the bird's bill and the clam. Sensing that slight pressure, the bird knows that probing in that direction might be worthwhile.

■ The Sanderling is the sandpiper best adapted to sandy beaches and can be seen by beach-going humans on the East and West Coasts. They have evolved a strategy to use waves to find food. An incoming wave rushes up the beach, stirring up the sand and sending the birds in a quick dash to escape the rising water. As soon as the wave retreats, though, they run back after it, looking for any invertebrates, like clams or sand crabs, that have been uncovered by the moving water, and they stop to feed. A few seconds later, the next wave forces them to dash uphill again, and the process repeats.

■ High-speed video taken of phalaropes shows that they can transport their prey from bill tip to mouth in as little as 0.01 second. That's about thirty times faster than the blink of an eye.

A Wilson's Phalarope manipulating food into its mouth

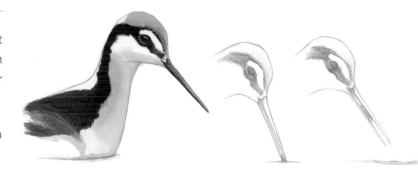

American Woodcock

SNIPE AND WOODCOCK

Spending most of its time alone in the forest, the woodcock emerges at
dawn and dusk in spring to perform a spectacular courtship flight.

To impress mates and rivals, the snipe does not use its voice to sing; instead, it produces a humming whistle with its tail. This is easy to observe, but some of the details of how the physics work were only recently revealed by research. The trailing edge of the outermost tail feathers is lighter colored and lacks barbules (hooks) to hold the vane together, making that edge of the feather less stiff. When these feathers are extended perpendicular to the body at high speed, the trailing edge of the feather can flutter very rapidly, like a flag in high wind, and its shape and flexibility is "tuned" to vibrate at the frequency that produces the low whistling sound of the snipe's display.

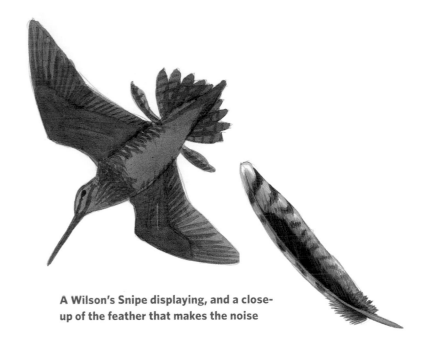

A Wilson's Snipe displaying, and a close-up of the feather that makes the noise

The snipe hunt is a practical joke, popular in the United States as early as the 1840s. An unsuspecting newcomer is invited on the hunt, given a bag, and led to a remote location with instructions for catching a mysterious swamp creature called a snipe. Recommended techniques include holding the bag open and just waiting, or making odd noises to attract the snipe into the bag, especially at night. The pranksters then leave the newcomer alone in the woods, "holding the bag." There is a real bird called a snipe—a chunky sandpiper that hides in wet muddy and grassy areas, relying on its cryptic coloration for camouflage. No one has ever caught a snipe in a bag.

A Wilson's Snipe in the grass

Birds generally have excellent eyesight. Their field of vision—the spread of surroundings they can see all at once—greatly surpasses that of humans. Human eyes are positioned to focus together on a single point. If we hold still, we can see about half of our surroundings (although we see detail in only one tiny point at the center of our vision). The snipe, like many other sandpipers and ducks, can see the entire 360 degrees around, and a full 180 degrees overhead—all at the same time. And instead of seeing a small area in fine detail, they see detail in a wide horizontal band in each eye! Imagine seeing the entire sky and horizon without turning your head. This is critical for birds like snipes that rely on camouflage for protection. Their first response to approaching danger is simply to crouch and freeze, and while remaining perfectly motionless, they can still see everything around them.

Front view of a Wilson's Snipe

GULLS

Gulls may be the most versatile birds in the world. In a bird triathlon—swim, run, fly—gulls would be among the favorites to win. Other birds may swim faster, run faster, and fly faster, but no other bird does all three so well. This versatility allows gulls to take advantage of a very wide range of feeding opportunities.

Ring-billed Gulls raiding a picnic at the beach

Gulls are notorious for eating junk. Literally. They flock to open garbage dumps to scavenge food, and they hang around outside picnic sites and restaurants, ready to gulp down any scraps. Despite this, they are careful about what they feed their chicks. Many studies have shown that when the chicks hatch, they are provided with highly nutritious natural food like crabs and fresh fish, even as their parents visit the garbage dump to feed themselves.

A Herring Gull regurgitating food for its chicks

The outer wing feathers of most gulls are gray with a black-and-white pattern at the tip. A new feather (top) has intact white markings; an old feather (bottom) has lost most of the white parts. Almost all gulls have dark pigment in their wing tips, and this is a common pattern across all families of birds. One reason is that melanin (the pigment responsible for black and brown colors) strengthens the feather, making it more resistant to wear and tear. The tip of the wing is crucial for flight so making it a little stronger is important.

What do birds do in a hurricane? Birds can sense barometric pressure, and when the pressure drops, indicating that a storm is coming, their first reaction is to start eating more. Their strategy for riding out a storm is usually to stock up on food, find some shelter, and just sit and wait. Shelter for a gull might be a clump of grass or a log on a beach, which provide protection from the wind. They will stand facing into the wind, with their heads down for streamlining. As long as they have some fat reserves, there is no need for them to move.

Herring Gulls hunkering down in a storm

TERNS

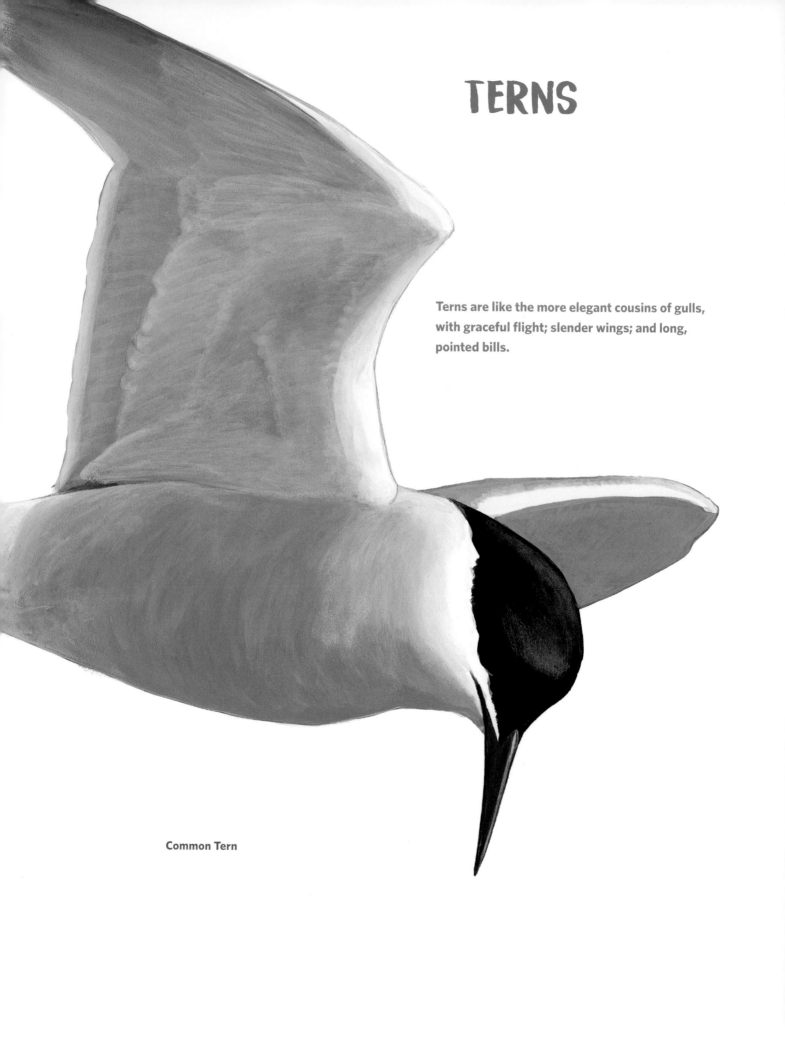

Terns are like the more elegant cousins of gulls, with graceful flight; slender wings; and long, pointed bills.

Common Tern

Why do some birds nest together in colonies? The disadvantages of living in crowded conditions include more exposure to disease and parasites and more competition (for food, nest sites, nest materials, and mates). But there are plenty of advantages: A larger colony can mount a much stronger attack against a predator than an isolated pair. Even when parents are absent from their own nest for long periods in search of food, the colony as a whole will still be defended by other colony members. A colony also functions as an information exchange, allowing birds to take advantage of food sources discovered by their neighbors. The chance of discovering small schools of fish is greatly increased with more birds searching. Once a school is discovered, other terns can quickly join the feeding frenzy.

A colony of Common Terns: Each pair defends a small space around their nest, but everything else is shared.

A Common Tern hovering and diving for fish

Finding fish in the open ocean is a challenge. Terns patrol at a low height, scanning for small fish. When they find fish close to the surface, they circle about ten feet over the water, picking their target and waiting for the right moment. Then they turn and drop straight into the water headfirst, hoping they can close their bills around a fish. They fly off immediately, and if they've captured a fish, they either swallow it while flying or carry it back to their nest. Along the way, they hope to avoid other birds that want to steal their fish.

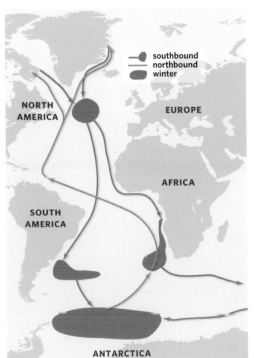

southbound
northbound
winter

NORTH AMERICA

EUROPE

AFRICA

SOUTH AMERICA

ANTARCTICA

Beginning at Arctic nesting sites, Arctic Terns migrate south (orange lines) to their Antarctic winter range (blue), then return north on a different route (green).

Terns are very strong fliers, and none more so than the Arctic Tern. It lives most of the year in sunlight, traveling from Arctic summer to Antarctic summer, and it spends most of the year near icebergs. Terns are not great swimmers, so they're on the wing for months at a time. Their migration route is not a straight line, but takes wide loops around the ocean. An individual bird might travel sixty thousand miles in a year—extraordinary!

HAWKS

If you see a large hawk perched along a road or field edge anywhere in North America, it's likely a Red-tailed Hawk.

A Red-tailed Hawk hunting along a roadside

■ The overall color of birds varies and can change seasonally or with age, or it can be different between males and females. A few species, including the Red-tailed Hawk, show color morphs. That means an individual is either dark or light overall and will remain that way its whole life. Recent research suggests that (at least in hawks) this kind of variation is related to camouflage. Dark-morph birds are less visible—and therefore more successful at capturing prey—in low light (as in forests). Light-morph birds are more successful in brighter light (as in open areas). Each color morph has an advantage under different conditions.

**Dark-morph and light-morph
Red-tailed Hawks**

Red-tailed Hawk kiting and stooping

■ Red-tailed Hawks are patient hunters, often sitting for hours on a branch or pole where they have a good view of their surroundings, watching for an opportunity. They will also spend hours in the air—kiting (hanging stationary in the breeze with little or no flapping), soaring, or gliding over open areas, watching for prey on the ground. They take mainly small mammals, like small rodents and squirrels, but any animal up to the size of a small rabbit is fair game.

■ Most species of birds don't vary much in size. They reach adult size within a few weeks of hatching, and after that, all individuals are a similar size. In most species of birds, males are slightly larger than females. In most hawks (and owls and hummingbirds), however, the opposite is true—females are larger than males. The female does most of the incubation, and her larger body mass may possibly make it easier for her to keep the eggs and young chicks warm. At the same time, the male's smaller size makes him quicker and more agile, allowing him to grab smaller prey as he finds food. After the eggs hatch, both male and female hunt for the family, and being different sizes might allow them to capture a wider range of prey.

**The larger and bulkier female Red-tailed Hawk (left)
and the smaller male (right)**

49

The nesting cycle of the Red-tailed Hawk

Nest-building begins sometime between January and April, depending on the climate. Both male and female gather materials, carrying sticks in their bills, but the female does most of the work shaping the nest. The process takes between four and seven days. They work mainly in the morning, being stealthy to keep the location secret.

Egg-laying might not begin for three to five more weeks. Usually only two or three eggs are laid, sometimes four. Typically, an egg is laid every other day. Incubation begins as soon as the first egg is laid and is performed mostly by the female. The male helps a bit with incubation and brings food to the female on the nest. Incubation lasts twenty-eight to thirty-five days.

Red-tailed Hawks leave the nest (fledge) at forty-two to forty-six days after hatching, but they stay close to the nest and rely on the parents for almost all their food for two to three more weeks. They gradually capture more of their own food but continue to get some food from the parents for at least eight weeks after fledging. The chicks spend a lot of time during their last two weeks in the nest exercising their growing wings and begin proper soaring flight about four weeks after fledging. In migratory populations, adults and fledglings go their separate ways about ten weeks after fledging. In sedentary populations, the family can stay together for up to six months.

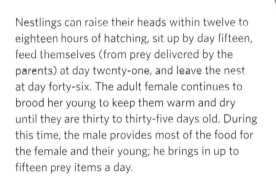

Nestlings can raise their heads within twelve to eighteen hours of hatching, sit up by day fifteen, feed themselves (from prey delivered by the parents) at day twenty-one, and leave the nest at day forty-six. The adult female continues to brood her young to keep them warm and dry until they are thirty to thirty-five days old. During this time, the male provides most of the food for the female and their young; he brings in up to fifteen prey items a day.

The first egg laid hatches first, and later eggs hatch with one to two days between. Because of this asynchronous hatching, the young are at different developmental stages, with a range of size and strength. If food is limited, the chicks compete for it in the nest. The strongest nestlings (usually the oldest) will get the most. The weakest will starve or even be eaten by their siblings. This system may seem cruel, but feeding the strongest chick first ensures the best outcome for the most chicks—it is better to raise one healthy chick than two malnourished ones.

ACCIPITERS

Cooper's Hawk

Predators inspire fear, which can cause their prey to change their usual behavior.

■ With long tails and short, powerful wings, the hawks in the genus *Accipiter* are excellent fliers and can move easily through tangled branches and obstacles. *Accipiters* specialize in hunting small birds—yes, some birds eat other birds! It can be shocking to witness, but it is important to remember the critical role that predators play in ecology. Small birds shelter in fear when an *Accipiter* shows up—which then creates an opportunity for their prey (insects, seeds, and so on) to survive in the areas that those small birds are avoiding. Predators control the populations of their prey species, and even that species' prey—all of which has far-reaching effects on the entire natural world.

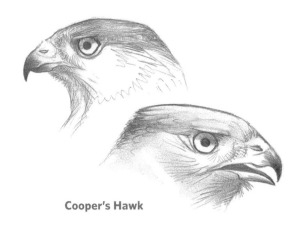

Cooper's Hawk

Cooper's Hawk stalking a Black-capped Chickadee

■ For centuries, humans considered hawks to be evil predators and persecuted them. Educational campaigns in the late 1800s and early 1900s showed the value of hawks and the important role they play in the human ecosystem, too (for example, they help protect farmers' crops by eating mice). This information led to strict laws to protect hawks. But hawks are still thought to be villains in many areas, and this same thinking continues unfairly in attitudes toward wolves and other large predators.

■ Along with their very sharp eyesight and wide field of view, birds process visual information much faster than humans do. Movies are a series of still images flashing by at about thirty pictures per second. This is too quick for our vision to capture, and the images blur together into a "moving picture." Birds can process images more than twice as fast as we can, so they would actually see one of our movies as a slideshow. This ability allows them to dodge obstacles and track prey during high-speed flight. Where we see signposts on the highway passing in a blur, a bird could still see details of each post.

■ Alert and quick, the Cooper's Hawk and its close relative the Sharp-shinned Hawk both live on small birds. These species often hunt around bird feeders in winter. They hide behind hedges or fences, then suddenly burst into the open. In that fraction of a second, they look for a songbird that is slow, inattentive, or just unlucky. With a quick flick of its wings and tail, the hawk spins to follow the smaller bird, trying to get close enough that its long legs and needle-sharp talons can reach out and snare the prey.

Sharp-shinned Hawk with songbird prey

EAGLES

Bald Eagles were endangered in the
1970s, due to DDT and other threats,
but now, with protection, the species is
again widespread.

Bald Eagle

■ We call someone "eagle-eyed" if they spot very distant objects. Eagles react to distant events that we can see only with the aid of binoculars, like a rabbit hopping on a hillside a mile away. Eagles have five times as many light-sensing cells packed into their eyes—so they can see a lot more detail than we can. And almost all those cells (80 percent) are cones that see color. We have only 5 percent color-sensing cones and 95 percent rods (cells for dark-light vision). We can look through 5x binoculars to approximate an eagle's visual acuity, but we have no way to simulate their color vision.

Because of the position of the fovea, this Bald Eagle is looking directly at you (with one eye).

A Bald Eagle, showing the lines of sight of the four foveae

ACTIVITY

Look at a single word in this sentence and then try to read the words around it without moving your eyes. That tiny area of detail in the center of your vision is because of the fovea, a small pit in the retina of each eye where light-sensing cells are more tightly packed. We have one fovea in each eye; both eyes focus on the same point, and we see one spot of detail. Most of our visual field, over 110 degrees, is viewed by both eyes (this is called "binocular vision"). Eagles, however, have two foveae in each eye, for a total of four, and they all point in different directions. An eagle sees four areas of detail at all times, as well as nearly 360 degrees of peripheral vision! One fovea in each eye is aimed almost straight ahead, while the other points out at about 45 degrees. To look up at the sky or down to the ground, a bird will cock its head to one side, using one fovea of one eye to study something.

■ One of the most serious threats now facing eagles and many other birds is lead poisoning. Eagles swallow lead bullets that are found in prey (those already shot by hunters) or eat waterfowl that have high levels of lead (from swallowing lost or discarded lead fishing weights). Because a bird's digestive system relies on a muscular gizzard (stomach) and strong acids to pulverize and dissolve food, harder materials like rocks, seeds, bones, or metal fragments are simply ground up until they are small enough to pass through. This means that bits of lead can remain in the gizzard, breaking down and releasing lead into the body for many days. Signs of severe lead poisoning include weakness, lethargy, and green feces. All this lead comes from humans, and simply using alternatives to lead in ammunition and fishing weights would solve this problem.

This Bald Eagle is suffering from severe lead poisoning and needs treatment to have any chance of survival.

VULTURES

Turkey Vultures are nature's cleanup crew. They search for dead animals, using sight and smell while they fly, then drop down to land for a meal (their unique gut bacteria, which would be toxic to most other animals, helps them digest dead or rotten flesh).

Turkey Vulture

Vultures spend the night roosting in large groups in trees or on buildings. In the early morning, they often stand with their wings spread and their backs to the sun. On cool mornings, this may help dry off any dew that collected on their wings during the night—which would reduce any extra weight and make flight easier.

Turkey Vultures roosting with wings spread

The low and slow flight of Turkey Vultures allows them to use their sense of smell to find food.

You might have heard that birds cannot smell, but all birds can! Turkey Vultures have a powerful sense of smell. It is common to see Turkey Vultures flying relatively low—around treetop level—presumably hunting by both sight and smell. A related species called the Black Vulture has a weaker sense of smell and often locates food by following Turkey Vultures.

Flying is a lot of work! Birds try to save energy when they fly and have many tricks to stay aloft without flapping. Riding updrafts to gain altitude is one. Here's how they work: Bare ground—like fields or parking lots—absorbs heat from the sun. As air near the ground warms up, it rises. This creates a column of rising warm air—a *thermal*—that reaches hundreds or even thousands of feet high. A soaring bird can sense the air movement and fly in circles to stay in the column. It simply fans its wings and tail and lets the rising air carry it up like an elevator. When it reaches the top, the bird bends its wings and glides in the direction it wants to travel, searching for the next thermal.

Turkey Vultures have evolved the ability to ride updrafts and thermals with almost no effort, so they can stay in the sky for hours. Their flight is distinctive—they fly with the wings raised in a V (dihedral) and constantly tilt from side to side as they react to air currents. They can tilt away from an updraft that is too strong, spilling air from one wing while allowing the other wing to provide lift and push them back upright. In this way, they can fly low and slow in search of food, staying airborne with only tiny adjustments of their wings, where other species would need to flap frequently to regain their balance.

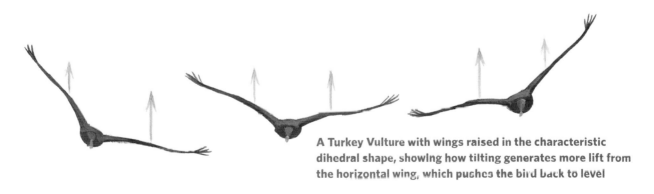

A Turkey Vulture with wings raised in the characteristic dihedral shape, showing how tilting generates more lift from the horizontal wing, which pushes the bird back to level

FALCONS

An American
Kestrel eating a
grasshopper

One of the smallest falcons in
the world, this species nests
in old woodpecker holes, dead
trees, and other cavities.

■ The intricate color pattern on the American Kestrel includes two false eye spots on the back of the head. This creates the illusion of a face and is an example of *deflective coloration.* Would-be predators are fooled by the false face and think they are being watched, or they are uncertain about which way the kestrel is facing, which causes them to either delay or give up an attack. (Yes, small hawks and falcons can be prey for larger species.)

■ The American Kestrel, related to the Peregrine Falcon, eats grasshoppers and mice. Kestrels can still be seen in open country, often perched on wires or fences along roadsides or hovering over fields as they hunt, but few people see them regularly. The population has been declining for decades, and their grumpy *"killy killy killy"* call is no longer a familiar sound. Reasons for the decline are still unknown, but it may be related to a few things: the loss of farmland habitat, the increased use of insecticides on farms and lawns, or the loss of nest sites (as fewer large, dead trees are left standing).

A Peregrine Falcon in a high-speed dive, or "stoop"

■ The Peregrine Falcon is the fastest animal in the world. It is capable of speeds of at least 242 miles per hour (and potentially more than 300 miles per hour) and can make turns that generate 27 Gs (one G is the force of gravity, and humans lose consciousness at 9 Gs). Peregrines usually circle high overhead when hunting. When they see potential prey—such as a duck—they fold their wings and go into a steep dive, called a "stoop." The falcon surprises its prey, hitting it with its feet from above. The impact of being struck by a two-pound falcon traveling at over 200 miles per hour stuns or kills the duck instantly. The duck falls to the ground, and the falcon circles back to settle and feed.

Blue lines show a thermal of warm air rising from the open field; the reddish spiral shows the path of a Peregrine Falcon entering low and circling to ride the rising air upward.

OWLS

The most widespread owl, found in every
state and province in North America

Great
Horned
Owl

■ The "horns" of the Great Horned Owl are actually tufts of feathers on its head. They may resemble ears or horns, but they are formed by just a few feathers and can be raised or lowered depending on the owl's mood. The function of these tufts is unknown, but it's possible that they are used for courting displays or for camouflage.

Barn Owl turning its head to hear you better

■ Wherever you live, chances are a Great Horned Owl lives within a few miles. This species has proved to be very adaptable and has taken advantage of the many small mammals that live in suburbia. Where Red-tailed Hawks hunt in the day, Great Horned Owls hunt at night. On average, 90 percent of their diet is mammals—but the diet of some can be up to 90 percent birds, mainly waterfowl or medium-size birds roosting in the open, also nestlings, and even some smaller owls.

■ There's a common myth that owls can spin their heads completely around. This is not quite true, but they can turn 270 degrees in either direction, three-quarters of a full circle (and *all* birds can turn more than halfway around). An owl has twice as many vertebrae in its neck as we do, which is one of the things that make its neck more flexible. By twisting their heads into odd positions they are turning their ears to test the sound from different angles and get a better fix on a location.

An Eastern Screech-Owl roosting in a hollow tree

■ Owls have extremely sensitive hearing. Some have even adapted to hunt almost entirely by sound. In the Barn Owl, the outer ear flaps are asymmetrical: The left ear opening is higher and angled downward, while the right ear opening is lower and angled upward. The ear angled downward captures more sound from below, and the ear angled upward captures more sound from above. The ears angled upward and downward allow owls to pinpoint the height of a sound, not just the direction, unlike our ears. Interestingly, asymmetrical ears have evolved independently in at least four different owl species, each time in a slightly different way.

A Barn Owl, showing the different position and direction of the two ears

A wing feather (left) and body feather (right) of a Great Horned Owl

■ Owls' wing feathers have several adaptations for silent flight, including a downy or velvety upper surface. Softer, more flexible feathers allow air to flow smoothly around the wing, reducing turbulence and noise. These same adaptations also reduce the noise of feathers brushing against each other as the wing moves. Besides the wing feathers, the body feathers of owls are also soft and fuzzy. As the owl's body feathers slide across each other (when turning the head in a circle, for example), they are silent. Imagine how quiet your movements are when wearing a soft sweater instead of a crinkly nylon rain jacket. This has two advantages: It makes it harder for prey to sense the owl's presence, and it allows the owl to hear the noises around it more clearly.

■ Even with their excellent hearing, most owls still require some vision to capture prey. Barn Owls, though, can capture prey in total darkness, using sound alone. Experiments have shown that Barn Owls can pinpoint the location of a mouse from thirty feet away, strictly by sound, then fly to that exact spot even if the mouse makes no further sound. Barn Owls can determine the precise direction to their prey because of their ear adaptations. But how do they know the distance? And once they leave their perch—in total darkness—how do they track their progress in the air and land precisely on a tiny mouse thirty feet from their starting point? These are unanswered questions.

A Barn Owl striking a mouse

■ The Eastern Screech-Owl is common in woodland edges in the eastern parts of the continent, and the similar Western Screech-owl is found in the West. Most owls are active at night and shelter and rest during the daytime, often using the same perch every day. The velvety surface and soft edges of owl feathers are not as water-repellent as typical feathers, so they tend to get wet in the rain. This could be one reason that so many owls seek shelter in hollow trees or dense vegetation. Their cryptic colors, feather patterns, and ear tufts provide camouflage, allowing them to hide. Still, other birds or squirrels may discover a roosting owl and mob it. If you find a roosting owl, it is important to avoid disturbing it. Watch from a distance, and don't stay in the area long.

TURKEYS

A male Wild Turkey in full display

■ No other North American bird has such a complex history with humans. The Wild Turkey, which is its official name, is both a symbol of the wild, bountiful forests of the Americas and one of the most widely domesticated birds in the world. It was first domesticated in southern Mexico as early as 300 BC and brought back to Europe in 1519 by Spanish colonizers. Turkeys were very popular. People traded them between towns, and they spread quickly across Europe, reaching England in the 1540s.

A female Wild Turkey (front) reviews three displaying males

When colonizers set sail for Massachusetts on the *Mayflower* in 1620, several live turkeys were among the cargo, returning to the Americas 101 years after their ancestors were brought to Europe. At that time, Wild Turkeys were still common in North America, but by 1672—only fifty years later—it was rare to see one, and by 1850 the species was completely gone from much of the eastern United States. It was more than one hundred years before the species returned, thanks to efforts by wildlife managers, the regeneration of forests, and decreased hunting. Wild Turkeys rebounded in the late 1900s and are now a common sight.

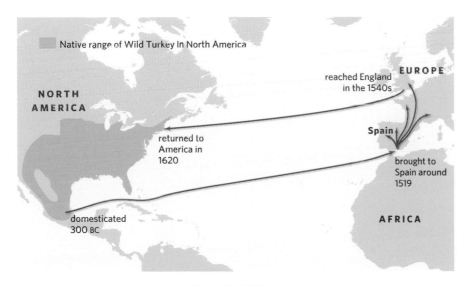

Native range of Wild Turkey in North America

NORTH AMERICA

EUROPE

reached England in the 1540s

Spain

returned to America in 1620

brought to Spain around 1519

domesticated 300 BC

AFRICA

The strange journey of the domesticated Wild Turkey

■ A bird's ears are on the side of the head behind and below the eye. In most species, the ear is hidden under specialized feathers. On birds like the Wild Turkey, which has no feathers on its head, the ear opening is clearly visible.

A female Wild Turkey

■ Wild Turkeys, like many species in the chicken family, do their courting display in a clearing called a lek so females can get a good view. Males hang around there in the spring, competing for the best positions. Females pass through, browsing the selection of available males and judging their displays. Females need to mate only once and have no further contact with the male. The female alone builds a nest, lays eggs, and raises the young.

GROUSE AND PHEASANTS

This subspecies of the Greater Prairie-Chicken was common in the northeastern states before 1800, including near Boston and New York City, but went extinct in 1932.

The Heath Hen

The largest muscles in a bird's body are the breast muscles that power flight. Two separate muscles are involved: one for the upstroke, one for the downstroke. On human bodies, the muscles for bringing our arms forward (downstroke) are on our chest, while the muscles for bringing our arms backward (upstroke) are on our back. Birds have evolved to have both muscles on the front, below the wings, for better weight balance in flight. This sketch shows how the larger downstroke muscles (darker red) attach to the underside of the wing to pull it down, and the upstroke muscles (lighter red) wrap over the shoulder and attach to the top of the wing like a pulley system. When you carve a chicken or turkey breast for dinner, you might notice the separation of these two large muscles.

Ring-necked Pheasant with breast muscles highlighted

ACTIVITY

Birds have many adaptations that make flight possible. Weight balance is one of the most important. A bird's heavier bones and muscles are all close together, in a dense, central mass below the wings. Wing and leg bones are controlled by long tendons connected to muscles in the compact body. The neck and head are very light, with a lightweight bill instead of heavy jaws and teeth. Try making a paper airplane, then tape a coin to different parts of the plane—the front, bottom, just one side. It will fly properly only if the extra weight is below the wings and near the center—just like in birds.

Ring-necked Pheasant with actual flesh and bones shown in red; the wings and tail are mostly feathers

Domestic chickens

What's the most common bird in North America? That would be the domestic chicken, with over two billion birds. About 500 million lay the eggs found in grocery stores and markets, and the rest have been raised for meat. That's about five times more than the human population of the continent! In contrast, the best guess for the most numerous wild bird in North America is the American Robin, at an estimated 300 million birds. That's slightly smaller than the human population.

67

QUAIL

Quail tend to be secretive and stay hidden in dense brush, though males often stand in the open to broadcast their call.

A male California Quail

The Northern Bobwhite is named for the male's call, a clear, cheerful whistle: "*bob-WHITE*." It is the only quail native to eastern North America. In the mid-1800s, hunting had reduced bobwhite numbers severely. By the mid-1900s, as farmland was converted into suburbs, their habitat and numbers had reduced even more. That trend continues, and populations now are less than 10 percent of what they were just sixty years ago.

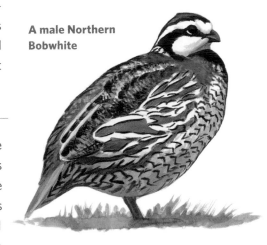

A male Northern Bobwhite

In response to declines, beginning in the mid-1800s, millions of bobwhite were trapped and moved from areas where they were still common (such as Mexico) to areas where they were declining (such as New England). Many more have been raised in captivity and then released into the wild. Introducing birds that are unfamiliar with or unsuited to the local conditions may have contributed further to local declines. The species can still be found in many states, but its long-term future in the wild is uncertain.

A California Quail scratching

Birds spend a lot of their time searching for food. Finding food on the ground often means having to sift through leaves and dirt. Quail (like their close relative the chicken) have evolved a one-footed scratch maneuver to help uncover food. They stand on one leg and kick backward with the other leg, scratching their toes along the surface and sending leaves and dirt flying backward. They can't see what their feet are doing, though, so, to look for food, they have to stop scratching, take a half step backward, and study the ground.

The feathers on a bird grow in a very organized arrangement, like shingles on a roof. Even the slightest incremental changes in each feather—in the background color, or the thickness and color of the shaft streak—can create amazing color patterns that are extremely complex yet pleasingly predictable.

California Quail belly feathers

PIGEONS

This species adapted to living around humans thousands of years ago, and now thrives in cities worldwide.

Rock Pigeons on a city ledge

■ Birdbrain, silly goose, dodo . . . these expressions and others reflect our low opinion of the intelligence of birds, but this is unfair to the birds. Crows and parrots perform as well as dogs in tests of reasoning and learning. Birds are self-aware and can learn by watching the experiences of other birds. Pigeons understand concepts like the difference between water in droplets, puddles, or lakes. They have even been trained to distinguish impressionist art from other styles, and to read mammograms as well as a human can. Overall, pigeons' ability to thrive in cities around the world requires cleverness and innovation, both signs of intelligence.

Rock Pigeon

■ With their remarkable navigational abilities, pigeons have been used to carry messages for thousands of years. Much of what scientists have learned about how birds navigate has been learned from studying pigeons. Pigeons can find their way back home from at least 2,500 miles away. How can they do what humans do, without a map and compass? The birds must have a form of inner GPS, with multiple senses and systems contributing. The picture that has emerged is complex. Pigeons sense the magnetic field, read the stars, track the sun, hear infrasound (very low-frequency noises), follow smells, and more— all integrated with a precise clock. And once they have experience with a route, they can follow the same path using rivers, hills, roads, buildings, and other landmarks.

A Rock Pigeon's normal cruising speed is nearly fifty miles per hour

■ Upon hearing the name *pigeon*, most people frown and think of the common Rock Pigeon of cities, which has evolved to live with humans. In the wild, Rock Pigeons roost and nest on cliff ledges, so adapting to the ledges of human structures like buildings and bridges was not hard for them. They originated in Europe, but there are other species of pigeons native to North America. The most widespread is the beautiful and majestic Band-tailed Pigeon, found in the mountains of the western United States. Another native pigeon is, sadly, extinct. The Passenger Pigeon was once considered the most abundant bird in North America, traveling in flocks of hundreds of millions of birds. They nested together in huge colonies wherever food was abundant. In the mid-1800s, with cities growing in the eastern United States, and new railroads making transportation and trade easier, entire nesting colonies were sold for food. The last Passenger Pigeon died in a zoo in 1914.

The native Band-tailed Pigeon

71

DOVES AND PIGEONS

Two Mourning Doves waiting out a snowstorm

Birds generally find as much shelter as they can and conserve energy during extreme weather.

Pigeons and doves are closely related. Along with the American Robin, the Mourning Dove is one of the most widespread species across North America. Part of why they are so successful is their ability to nest almost year-round (from March to October), even in chillier northern climates. By contrast, most species in the northern states have a very limited nesting season of less than two months.

A Rock Pigeon walking: the head remains stationary while the body moves forward

Many birds bob their heads back and forth as they walk, and they do it to help keep their vision fixed on their surroundings. Head bobbing is synchronized with foot movements. As one foot is picked up and moved forward, the head snaps forward and then remains nearly stationary while the body moves forward below it. As the trailing foot is picked up off the ground, the head snaps forward again, and the cycle repeats.

Mourning Dove partly asleep

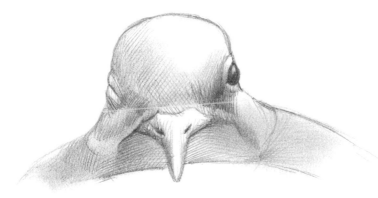

Can birds really sleep with one eye open? Yes! Bird sleep is quite different from ours, and they can put half of their brain to sleep while continuing activity with the other half. We could say this dove is "half asleep," but research shows that it is really about three-quarters asleep. The side of the brain with the eye open is really in an intermediate state, resting while still watching for danger.

The Mourning Dove's mournful hooting call is often mistaken for an owl's. But why do their wings make a whistling sound on takeoff? Researchers played recordings of this whistling sound for doves and other birds to test their reactions. Scientists found that the sound of a normal, relaxed takeoff caused no reaction, but the sound of a panicked takeoff (higher pitched and with quicker wingbeats) caused doves and other birds to flee in alarm. Clearly the wing whistle of doves can be a signal alerting other birds to potential danger.

Mourning Dove taking off

HUMMINGBIRDS

Male hummingbirds will fiercely defend a patch of flowers (or feeders) against all other hummers.

Male Rufous Hummingbirds battling over a patch of flowers

Many species of birds have shimmery, iridescent colors, which are produced by the microscopic structure of the feathers' surface. The iridescent colors of the throat of a male hummingbird are among the most spectacular colors in all of nature. The structure of the feather surface boosts one color of light, and the surfaces are angled so that they reflect that shimmering color in only one direction: straight ahead of the bird. A male hummingbird as shown here can look black-headed most of the time. Only when it turns to face you directly can you see the way the throat glows with an intense beam of brilliantly colored light.

Male Ruby-throated Hummingbird in side view and front view

A torpid Rufous Hummingbird

Smaller hummingbird species (including Rufous Hummingbird) beat their wings over seventy times a second. That adds up to over 250,000 wingbeats per hour, and over a million wingbeats in just four hours of flying. In a year, a single bird beats its wings well over half a billion times! It takes a lot of fuel to keep a hummingbird going at its normal pace, and it needs to feed constantly during the day. To conserve energy to get through a long night with no food, hummingbirds can slow down their body processes, becoming torpid. During torpor, the tiny bird's body temperature can drop below 60°F. The heart rate can slow from five hundred beats per minute to fewer than fifty, and breathing may briefly stop. How do hummingbirds come out of torpor? As their heart and breathing rates rise, their flight muscles shiver and their wings begin to vibrate. The use of any body muscles generates heat. (This is also true in mammals, which is why we get hot while exercising and shiver when we're cold to keep warm.) The heat generated by the vibrating wing muscles warms the hummer's blood supply. The warmed blood circulates throughout the body, and soon the hummer's body temperature is back up to its normal toasty range of 100 to 104°F.

Hummingbirds have long bills but very short legs relative to body size. They can't walk or hop—every movement requires flying. Hummingbirds can also hover in place. Their wings twist, which generates lift on both forward and backward strokes. Picture a helicopter for comparison: A helicopter's rotor blades (the blade that spins at the top of the craft) lift the helicopter because they are angled. The leading edge of the blade (the part that contacts the wind first) is higher so that as the blades spin, they create higher air pressure below the blade. Hummingbird wings work the same way, except they can't spin in a complete circle around the bird. Instead, they have to reverse direction and flap very quickly back and forth. In each direction, the wing twists so that the leading edge is higher and the movement of the wing pushes air down—which then pushes them up. Insects have near-perfect hovering efficiency; they generate an equal amount of lift on both the forward and backward wing strokes. Hummingbirds, on the other hand, get only about 30 percent of their lift from the backward stroke. Larger birds, like the Belted Kingfisher, do not truly hover. They usually require some wind to help keep them in place.

Traveling forward (reddish), the wing twists so that the leading edge is higher; traveling backward (bluish), the wing twists the other way so that again the leading edge is higher.

MORE HUMMINGBIRDS

The largest hummingbird found north of Mexico, and the smallest

Blue-throated Hummingbird (top) and Calliope Hummingbird (bottom)

■ Hummingbirds and flowers have evolved together. The flowers pollinated by hummingbirds are often perennial, red, tubular, and without strong odor. Hummers remember the locations of perennials (flowers that regrow every spring) to return to them every year. A narrow tube ensures that hummingbirds are the only creatures that can reach the nectar. Flowers also adjust their nectar content to lure hummingbirds back for repeated visits, which increases the flower's own chance of pollination.

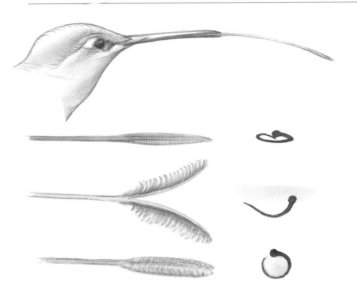

■ Hummingbirds feed by dipping their long, slender tongue into the nectar inside a flower. The tip of the tongue is forked. Each fork has a fringe that forms a flexible tube designed to hold liquid. The fringe spreads out when it is submerged in nectar, and wraps securely around a drop of nectar as it is pulled back into the bill. Inside the bill, the nectar is squeezed out and swallowed, and the tongue immediately dips into the flower again. This action can be repeated twenty times per second—a lot faster than a human can even count. All the bird has to do is extend its tongue into the flower and pull it back full of nectar, like dipping a paintbrush into water.

The hummingbird tongue on the left, and a magnified cross section on the right, shown as the tongue emerges from the bill (top), as it enters the liquid nectar (middle), and as it is pulled back into the bill (bottom)

ACTIVITY

Feeding hummingbirds is simple, and the birds are amazing to watch. There are just a few things to know. Use plain white sugar, dissolved in water at a ratio of about four parts warm tap water to one part sugar. White sugar is sucrose, the same as flower nectar. No brown sugar, organic sugar, or "raw" sugar! These can contain iron, which harms hummingbirds. Hummingbird feeders are red, like their favorite flowers, to attract the birds. The red parts of the feeder will draw the birds over, so there's absolutely no need to add food coloring to the water. Keep your feeders clean. Rinse them out and replace the nectar every few days (more often in warm weather) to stop mold or fungus from growing. If you have trouble with one dominant bird chasing away other hummingbirds, try putting out more feeders. A typical individual visits the feeder about once every thirty minutes, and in between, it will catch insects (which can constitute up to 60 percent of its diet) and visit flowers. A rough rule of thumb for estimating the total number of hummingbirds using your feeder is to count the most birds you see at one time and multiply that by ten.

Ruby-throated Hummingbirds at a feeder

ROADRUNNER

Roadrunners rely on quick reflexes and surprise to catch their prey. Running is mainly for travel.

A Greater Roadrunner with a lizard

A hypothetical race involving a roadrunner and four competitors

■ A roadrunner is faster than most humans. If the competitors shown here ran a 100-meter sprint, the ostrich would easily take first place, in under five seconds. The coyote would be close behind, in under six seconds. The roadrunner and Usain Bolt would take about twice as long. A roadrunner's top speed is said to be about 20 miles per hour, which would get it across the finish line in just over eleven seconds. Usain Bolt's 100-meter record is under 9.6 seconds, or about 23 miles per hour. The average human runner finishes in fifteen seconds (under 15 miles per hour). So an elite human sprinter would beat the roadrunner to the line—but most of us would not.

■ The roadrunner is one of the most iconic species of the American desert Southwest. In the cuckoo family, they spend most of their time on the ground, flying only reluctantly. They eat almost anything they can catch, from beetles and lizards to snakes and birds. Contrary to the classic cartoon, they are not at war with coyotes.

■ For more than a century, the link between birds and dinosaurs was debated. Recent discoveries have settled the debate: It's a fact that modern birds are the descendants of dinosaurs. Scientists have found dinosaur fossils with feathers and other birdlike features, and now we have a better sense of how feathers evolved since then. *Anchiornis* (an-chee-or-nis), shown here, was one of the earliest "proto-birds" from about 160 million years ago; it was smaller than a roadrunner. It probably couldn't fly. Its feathers were loose and shaggy, without those tiny interlocking barbules (which appeared during the fourth stage in the evolution of feathers). The feathers might have been useful for gliding but were probably mostly just for insulation and display. Many other feathered dinosaurs and true birds evolved in the next 100 million years after *Anchiornis*. Almost all of them went extinct after the meteor impact 66 million years ago.

The feathered dinosaur known as *Anchiornis*

■ That same meteor impact ended the Cretaceous period, the last era that dinosaurs roamed the earth. During that time, there was a great variety of birds. Many of those species lived in trees and were capable of flying. But the meteor impact killed most of the large trees on earth, as well as all the nonavian dinosaurs. In fact, only about 25 percent of all species of plants and animals survived the catastrophic global changes. Among birds, just a few small, ground-dwelling species survived. These included one species that gave rise to the modern tinamou/ostrich group, another species that gave rise to the modern duck/chicken group, and a third species (perhaps pigeon-like or maybe even roadrunner-like) that gave rise to all other modern birds.

Greater Roadrunner running

KINGFISHERS

This species is most often seen on a perch overlooking the water.

A Belted Kingfisher in a typical setting

■ Kingfishers catch fish by "hovering" and then diving headfirst into the water. If you watch a kingfisher while it is hovering, you'll notice that the head remains still in the air, holding a fixed position over the water, while the wings flap and the body does the work of flying. It's important for the bird to keep its head steady so that its eyes can remain fixed on a target below. The control needed for this is truly remarkable. Imagine standing on a rocking boat and keeping your head at a fixed point in space—that is just one part of what the kingfisher is doing while it hovers.

A Belted Kingfisher hovering

■ The kingfisher family includes more than three hundred species; only six of them are found in the Americas. As their name suggests, they mainly fish. But the remaining three-hundred-plus species are found in Asia, Australia, and Africa, and most of them do not eat fish. They are found in forests and brushy areas, where they eat insects and other small animals. The well-known kookaburra is a member of the kingfisher family.

A Belted Kingfisher near its nest— the hole in the bank

■ Ecologists talk about the concept of "limiting factors." This means that the entire population of a species can be limited by just one scarce resource. In the case of the Belted Kingfisher, that resource is nesting sites. While there are plenty of places for kingfishers to fish and feed themselves, there are fewer places for them to safely nest and reproduce.

They need a sandbank that's soft enough for the birds to burrow deep into, yet tall and steep enough to make it hard for predators to reach. As humans turn more and more rivers and streams into dams and channels, the right kind of sandbank is getting scarcer—and becoming a limiting factor in the population of Belted Kingfishers.

A kingfisher holds a very wiggly fish crosswise in the bill, whacks it hard against a branch to stop it from wiggling, then deftly tosses it in the air, catching it by the head and swallowing it headfirst.

Caught a fish... now what?

Birds have wings instead of hands and use their feet for perching. This means all food handling has to be done by the bill. Furthermore, they have no teeth, so prey must be swallowed whole. Imagine if your hands were tied behind your back and you had no teeth for chewing—how would you eat? Birds use their bills to manipulate their food and then swallow it whole, with the "chewing" stage happening in their muscular stomachs.

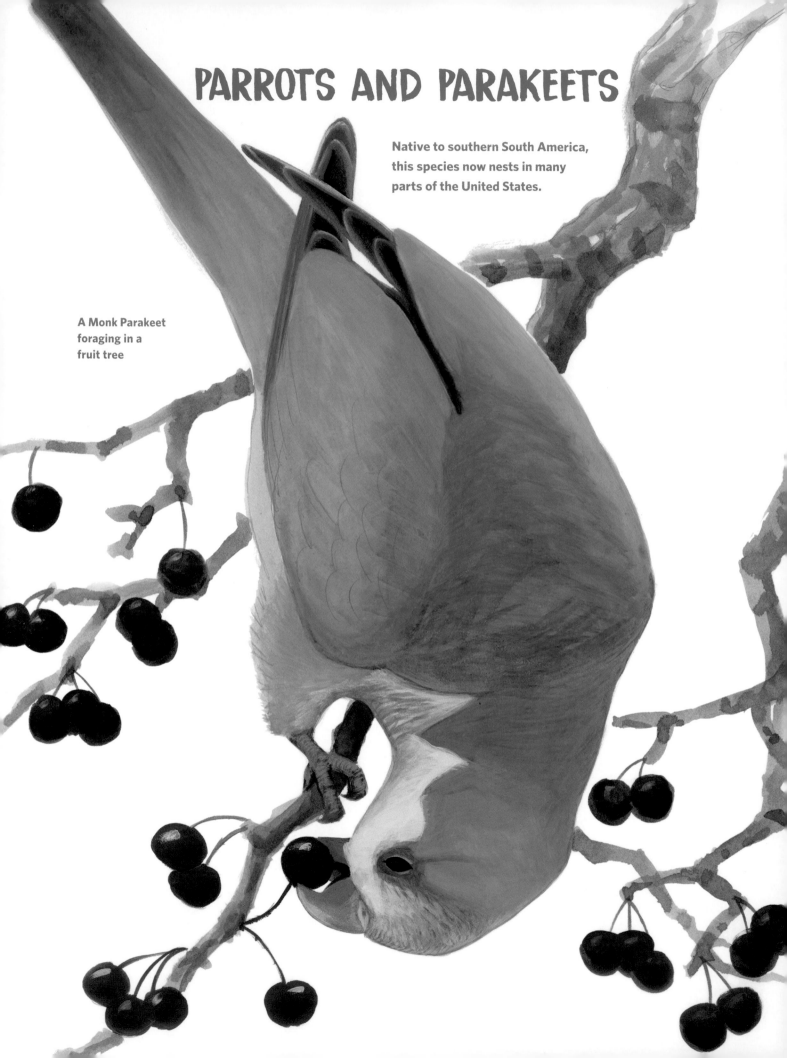

PARROTS AND PARAKEETS

Native to southern South America, this species now nests in many parts of the United States.

A Monk Parakeet foraging in a fruit tree

■ The brilliant green color of many parrot species is actually a combination of blue and yellow. The yellow is a pigment. The blue color, on the other hand, is a result of the microscopic structure of the feather, which relies partly on the blackish pigment melanin. The combination of the blue structural color and the yellow pigment is what produces the vibrant green.

Monk Parakeets: a typical bird (center) with one lacking melanin (right) and one lacking yellow pigment (left)

■ Without hands, most birds use their bills alone to manipulate food. Some species (for example, hawks, jays, and chickadees) use their feet to hold food while they pound or tear it with their bills. Only parrots use their feet to handle food. Interestingly, most species of parrots show a preference for one side (the same way humans are either righties or lefties) and most are left-footed. Research in parrots and humans suggests that performing tasks with only one side of the body promotes multitasking and creativity because it occupies only one side of the brain, leaving the other side free to do other things. This humanlike behavior is part of what makes parrots so unique and charming.

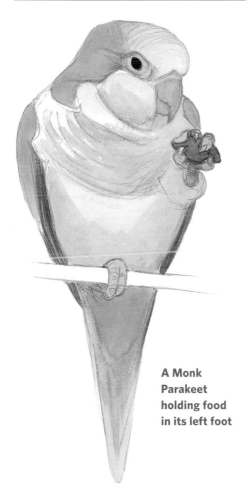

A Monk Parakeet holding food in its left foot

■ A bird's tongue helps it handle food. Parrots have a stubby, muscular tongues much like ours, and they use their tongues to help move food around in their mouths. There is also evidence that their tongues play a role in modifying sounds produced by the syrinx (birds' vocal organ), in the same way our tongues modify our voices. This may be one reason that parrots can mimic human speech so well.

A Monk Parakeet manipulating food with its tongue

■ The Monk Parakeet comes from South America and can survive as far north as Boston and Chicago. Many parrot species around the world are threatened with extinction. One reason is that humans have raided nests for young parrots that can be sold as pets—which has a devastating effect on their overall population. Many species have escaped from captivity and now survive in the wild in cities in the southern United States. Tragically, there are now more red-crowned parrots escaped from captivity and living wild in the southern United States than in the species' native range in Mexico. Only one species of parrot was native to the United States—the Carolina Parakeet, now extinct.

WOODPECKERS

These two similar species are found across North America; the Downy Woodpecker is smaller than the Hairy Woodpecker.

Downy Woodpecker (left) and
Hairy Woodpecker (right)

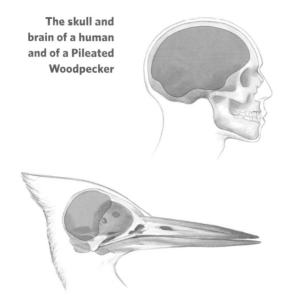

Woodpeckers engage in three very distinct activities that all involve banging on wood with their bills.

1. Drumming is the woodpecker's "song." It is performed mainly in the spring as a way of showing off to a mate or rival. A woodpecker sits in one spot and hammers its bill against wood in one short and very rapid burst. This produces lots of sound but does no damage to the wood.

■ Why don't woodpeckers get concussions from banging their heads against trees? Mainly because their brains don't weigh very much. Woodpeckers have several other adaptations that reduce the impact. One is that their brains have a wide surface facing the bill to absorb impact. Our brains are oriented to absorb impact from below (like jumping) but we are vulnerable to impact from front or back. Also, the lower mandible (the bottom part of the beak) is slightly longer. It strikes the wood first, transmitting the force through the lower jaw rather than into the skull. A layer of spongy bone at the base of the upper mandible also helps cushion any impact there.

2. A woodpecker foraging for food will move around, tapping and chipping, making lots of small holes as it seeks out insects in the wood. Foraging occupies a large part of each day, year-round.

■ The Downy Woodpecker and the Hairy Woodpecker both are common in woodlands across the United States and Canada, and they often visit feeders. The appearance of the Downy Woodpecker might be evolving to match the appearance of the Hairy Woodpecker, making it increasingly tricky for backyard birders to identify which is which. Recent research supports the idea that a smaller species (in this case, the Downy Woodpecker) can benefit when other birds mistake it for a larger, more dominant species (the Hairy Woodpecker) because it gets a higher position in the pecking order.

3. For its nest, a woodpecker knocks a neat round hole into a tree, then makes a larger cavity or hole inside the trunk. After a few days of work, the nest is large enough for the bird to climb inside.

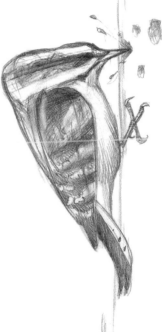

Downy Woodpecker drumming (top), foraging (center), and nest excavating (bottom)

A Yellow-bellied Sapsucker
with its sap wells

MORE
WOODPECKERS

■ There are four species of sapsuckers in the world, all in North America. These birds drill rows of shallow holes in trees, and return to drink the sap and to eat any insects that have been attracted. These sap wells make the nutritious sap available to any other birds and animals in the area as well—which leads ecologists to call sapsuckers a keystone species. Like the keystone at the very top of an arch, removing sapsuckers from an ecological community could cause the whole system to collapse.

■ The Acorn Woodpecker, found in the southwestern United States, has a unique habit: It drills small holes in trees and stores an acorn in each hole. This species lives in groups that all contribute to making holes and gathering acorns. Acorns are stored in the fall to be saved for the winter, when there isn't much other food available. This way, the birds can stay put through the winter and be healthy enough to breed in the spring. Holes are drilled in dead limbs or in thick bark so as not to hurt the tree, and they are reused each year. A typical storage tree has four thousand holes and could take over eight years to create—longer than most individual Acorn Woodpeckers live. The record—an estimated fifty thousand holes in one tree—probably took more than one hundred years altogether to make.

**A male Acorn Woodpecker
at its storage tree**

Red-bellied Woodpecker

■ Birds' ranges—where they nest, roost, eat, and more—have been shifting northward. For example, the Red-bellied Woodpecker—along with Northern Cardinal, Northern Mockingbird, Carolina Wren, and others—has settled in New England from the South within the last hundred years. Some of this is related to climate change. Milder winters allow birds to survive farther north. Human housing and buildings are also factors that affect birds. For example, houses and hedges create warm microclimates (small climates that are different from the surrounding area); planted shrubs and trees provide cover; and lots of bird feeders offer extra food.

FLICKERS

Because of the odd habits and bold markings of flickers, many people do not recognize them as a kind of woodpecker.

A Northern Flicker on the ground, eating ants

■ The most un-woodpecker-like woodpecker, flickers are often seen hopping around on lawns or in gardens, searching for their favorite food—ants. They are noisy in the spring and summer, giving a loud, clear *"keew"* and a long series of *"wik-wik-wik-wik"* notes. Flickers are much less common now than they were several decades ago—perhaps because there are fewer large, dead trees for nesting, fewer ants, or more pesticides, but the definite cause is unknown. By building nesting cavities in large, dead trees, flickers provide future nest sites for many other species, like the American Kestrel. The decline of flickers may therefore lead to the decline of populations of other species, too.

Northern Flicker displaying

■ When the Northern Flicker puts on its "dance" display, it stretches out its neck, fans its tail, and pivots its body side to side in time with a slow series of *"wikka"* calls. It does this when it's defending its territory or courting a mate.

"Red-shafted" Flicker (upper) and "Yellow-shafted" Flicker (lower)

■ The undersides of flickers' wings flash bright red or yellow in flight. "Red-shafted" Flickers are found mostly in the Rocky Mountains and West. "Yellow-shafted" Flickers occur in the East and North. Their color comes from carotenoid compounds, which are nutrients found in colorful fruits, vegetables, and autumn leaves. Carotenoids are processed differently by these two flicker species to result in either red or yellow pigment.

Northern Flicker taking off

■ When flickers take off, their bright white rump is visible. This, along with their red or yellow wings, probably serves to startle potential predators. The unexpected flash of bright color as the flicker bursts into flight might cause predators to hesitate—and increase the bird's chance of escape.

PHOEBES

Phoebes are small flycatchers that
have soft, whistled songs that say their
name—*"FEE-bee."*

**A Black Phoebe perched
on a lawn chair**

Many unrelated species of birds have a habit of pumping (or wagging) their tails, and many possible explanations have been offered. A recent study found that the rate of tail pumping increased only when a predator was close. Tail pumping tells the predator: "I know you're there. I'm healthy and quick, and you won't catch me, so don't even try." When humans get nervous, we fidget. When phoebes get nervous, they wag their tails, and when a predator sees fidgeting or tail wagging, it gets the message that this is a healthy, alert animal that may not be worth trying to chase. The behavior—fidgeting or twitching under stress—is universal, something we "just do" because it is instinctive.

Black Phoebe tail pumping

Most species of flycatchers are seen in forests, swamps, and dense brush. A few species are found in the open, and these include phoebes. Phoebes like to build their nests on protected ledges. Under the edge of a porch, they can find the perfect setting. Most songbirds will not reuse a nest, likely to avoid parasites. Phoebes are an exception, and they often reuse a nest more than once in a season or will reuse a nest from a previous year (with a little renovation).

Eastern Phoebe on a nest on a porch

Like most birds, phoebes generally swallow their prey whole, and the work of "chewing" is done in the muscular gizzard. Many insects have hard shell-like parts that cannot be digested. Small fragments will pass through a bird's intestines. Larger parts that can't be broken up, though, accumulate in the gizzard and are regurgitated (thrown up) as a small, compact pellet. Hawks and owls regurgitate pellets containing the bones and fur of their prey (about sixteen hours after a meal), and gulls produce pellets of fish bones. These bits of shell and bone in their diet also act as grit substitutes to help grind up the softer materials in the gizzard.

Black Phoebe regurgitating a pellet

MORE FLYCATCHERS

A Western Kingbird harassing a
Red-tailed Hawk

■ The Scissor-tailed Flycatcher has one of the most spectacular tails of any bird, but what is it for? Most birds have a tail because it improves flight performance and smooths the flow of air behind the body. A long, forked tail makes flight more efficient at high speed (when it is folded) and also at slow speed (when it is fanned). The Scissor-tailed Flycatcher's long and flashy tail, though, is mostly used for display and foraging. By flying slowly while dipping its tail into the grass, it can "sweep" insects out and catch them in flight.

Scissor-tailed Flycatcher "sweeping" with its tail

■ Kingbirds are larger, bolder, and more colorful flycatchers found in wide open spaces. They are agile yet aggressive, and they are known for defending their territory and nest against all intruders. They can attack any passing hawk from above and behind, often pecking at the back of the hawk's head, as shown in the image to the left.

■ All birds have extraordinary vision. Flycatchers certainly need it to catch tiny insects in flight. Imagine flying twenty miles per hour, swerving to follow the movements of a mosquito in flight, then grabbing that mosquito out of the air with a pair of tweezers. This requires several visual adaptations beyond human eyesight, including:

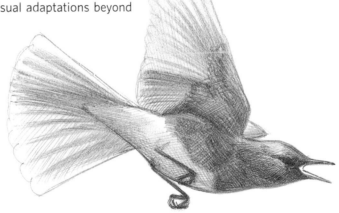

- The ability to see tiny specks at a distance.
- The ability to see ultraviolet light, which can help them to see insects against a background of leaves and shadows.
- Colored oil droplets inside cone cells in the eye, which can boost color definition. This makes it easier to pick out other colors against blue and green backgrounds.
- An ability to track very rapid movements (such as flying insects) even while flying at high speeds. Other birds process images more than twice as fast as we do, making high-speed motion less of a blur, and flycatchers have the fastest processing of any birds tested.

A Black Phoebe catching an insect

■ Rictal bristles are a set of whisker-like feathers around the base of the bill in flycatchers and several other families of birds. Experiments have shown that the bristles act as eye protection, a safety net that deflects insects (and their legs and wings) away from the eyes during high-speed capture.

A Willow Flycatcher with rictal bristles around the base of the bill

SWIFTS

Some species of swifts stay in the air
for ten months straight, every year!

A Chimney Swift high above the earth

■ Flight is essential to most birds' survival, and especially to swifts. They replace their large wing feathers every year to keep them in good shape. But how do these birds keep flying while they're growing new wing feathers? Like most birds, they replace their feathers gradually. They grow one or two new feathers at a time, enough to overlap and cover areas where old feathers have fallen out. The next feather won't drop until the growing feather is long enough to fill in, so there is never more than a small gap. This maintains a wing that can still fly. It can take more than three months for a Chimney Swift to complete the molt of all its flight feathers.

A Chimney Swift, showing the progression of new feathers (shown slightly darker) replacing old feathers, beginning with the inner feathers and moving gradually to the tip of the wing

■ Swifts' wings have a different structure from most other birds. They have much shorter "arm" bones, so most of their wing surface is made up of long feathers growing from the "hand" bones. The Ring-billed Gull, shown here in comparison, has longer "arm" bones, which allows it to change the shape of its wings to adjust to different conditions, simply by adjusting the angles of the wing bones. Swifts, on the other hand, have stiff, narrow wings that allow for fewer possible wing shapes. Generally, they fly straight and very fast, which is one reason they usually stay high in the open air. If they flew lower to the ground, it might be trickier for them to avoid obstacles with the same ease of other birds.

A Chimney Swift and a Ring-billed Gull (not to scale), with arm bones shown in blue and hand bones in red

■ The high, sharp twittering of Chimney Swifts is a common sound in eastern towns in the spring and summer, but you will never see one perched. Swifts are totally adapted to life up in the sky. These remarkable birds spend the entire day high in the air and spend the night inside chimneys. Before chimneys were common in houses and other human-made buildings, they would roost and nest in large, hollow trees. In September, they migrate to winter in South America. It's possible they stay in the air for the entire time, until they return to their nesting chimney the following April. Some other species of swifts are known to fly continuously over their wintering area, for about nine months, and it's possible that Chimney Swifts do the same. This means that they must sleep while flying! One study of frigatebirds (large seabirds that fly for days at a time) found that they don't sleep very much while flying, and usually only half of their brain is asleep, but sometimes they do fall completely asleep in flight.

Chimney Swifts dropping into a chimney

SWALLOWS

This species nests in barns. It is very rare to find a Barn Swallow nest that is not on a human structure.

A Barn Swallow hunting insects over a hayfield

Birds, overall, have evolved many styles for building nests. Groups of related bird species, though, tend to have a consistent nest style. Swallows are unusual in having a wide variety of nest styles, even among closely related species. Tree Swallows use old woodpecker holes or birdhouses and build a grass nest inside. Cliff Swallows make structures out of mud, then build a grass nest inside that. Some other swallows dig a tunnel into a sandbank and then build a grass nest inside. Barn Swallows nest on buildings and barns; in fact, it is rare to find a Barn Swallow nest that is *not* in some kind of human-made building. This species adapted to nesting in barns almost as soon as the structures were first built in the United States. The rapid spread of humans and barns in the 1800s probably allowed the Barn Swallow to greatly expand its nesting range.

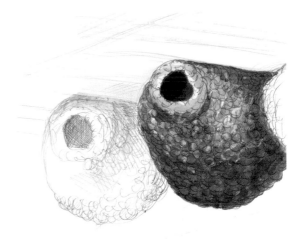

The half-bowl nest of a Barn Swallow (left) and the enclosed gourd-shaped nest of a Cliff Swallow (right). Both are built on a vertical wall, just below an overhang, using small mouthfuls of wet mud carefully stuck together and allowed to dry.

Barn Swallows in flight

Swallows fly for hours at a time. Sometimes they go low over fields, marshes, and ponds, and other times high in the air, catching small flying insects. This makes them part of a group of birds known as *aerial insectivores,* which also includes swifts, flycatchers, and others. Surveys in North America show that all these species have been declining over the last fifty years. One of the biggest reasons for this is probably a decline of insects. One possible cause of the decline of insects is the widespread use of insecticides in agriculture, on lawns, and more. Research, monitoring, and action are all urgently needed.

MORE SWALLOWS

Swallows often gather around wetlands,
where there are plenty of insects.

Tree Swallows roosting on reeds

■ Do birds return to the same territory every year? Almost certainly . . . if they survive the winter. Most species are loyal to their nesting site, especially if they were successful at raising young there. One study in Pennsylvania found that Tree Swallows returned to within a few miles of the nesting box where they were raised as chicks, and they made their own nesting attempts in the same area. Many birds similarly seek out familiar journeys and places; for example, many migratory species follow the same migration route and use the same winter territory each year, too.

A pair of Tree Swallows on a nesting box

■ Tree Swallows, like all swallow species, eat mainly insects that they capture in flight. This requires an abundance of small insects in the air—which happens only when the weather is good. When the air is too cold or damp for insects to fly (during a storm, for example), large numbers of swallows will rest together in reeds or bushes. They use torpor to slow down their body and conserve energy. They can survive for a few days with no food, but longer stretches of cold and damp weather can be a serious challenge.

A just-hatched Tree Swallow

■ All baby songbirds (such as this Tree Swallow) hatch naked, with eyes closed, and require constant feeding, warming, and protection by the parents to survive. These are known as altricial young. One advantage of having altricial young rather than precocial young is that the nesting female can lay smaller eggs that require fewer resources, since the eggs hatch at an earlier stage of development. But that simply delays the parenting work until later, and adult swallows have to invest a lot of time and energy to care for the young after they hatch.

CROWS

Crows travel in small groups year-round and are among the most intelligent birds.

An American Crow playing with a trinket

■ Intelligence is difficult to define—after all, it can mean many things. One indirect measure of intelligence is the ability to adapt and thrive in many different environments, to innovate. Ravens and crows are certainly some of the most intelligent and innovative birds. They also understand what trading is and have a sense of what makes a trade fair or unfair. In one study, human experimenters traded with ravens. Some humans were "fair" and traded items of equal value, while others were "unfair," giving a lower-quality item in exchange. The birds learned the tendency of each individual human and preferred to trade with the fair ones.

■ Crows' curious, sometimes destructive behavior (like opening trash bags in search of food) can make them seem nasty—but these are generally family groups in search of food, not trying to cause trouble. A typical group includes a breeding pair with their youngest offspring, as well as some older siblings. One-year-old crows usually stay with their parents to help raise their siblings, and some stay as long as five years!

A group of crows foraging

A juvenile American Crow

■ Baby crows—with partially grown feathers, pale bills, and blue eyes—tend to leave the nest early, often before they can really fly. Humans who find these baby crows on the ground sometimes try to "rescue" them, taking them in and feeding them for a few weeks until they are fully independent, but it's best to leave them alone. Most likely the parents are nearby and will take care of their baby. Also, social contact with other crows is important at this stage. Crows are clever and can be engaging and interesting pets, but they are wild animals and should be outdoors with their own kind. In fact, it can even be harmful to have humans as foster parents. One researcher tracked seven crows raised by humans, and none survived in the wild more than a few months after fledging. In contrast, more than half of young crows raised in the wild survive through their first winter.

■ Crows can recognize humans by our faces, and they associate each person with good or bad experiences. They can even communicate that information to other crows. One researcher who had trapped crows was still recognized by crows that had never been trapped, nearly a mile away from the trapping site and five years later! We can't recognize individual crows, but we can sometimes distinguish first-year birds from older crows. Adult crows have uniform glossy black feathers. Young crows have less glossy, matte black feathers, which become more faded and brownish through the winter.

A one-year-old (left) and adult (right) American Crow

RAVENS

Ravens are very closely related to crows and share the crows' intelligence and rich social life.

A bird can't preen its own head with its bill, so it uses its feet to clean head feathers. Ravens and some other species engage in mutual preening, in which birds help each other keep their head feathers clean and straight.

One of Aesop's fables, "The Crow and the Pitcher," tells the story of a thirsty crow that finds a pitcher with some water. The water is at the bottom of the pitcher, where the crow can't reach. By dropping pebbles into the pitcher, the bird is able to raise the water level and get a drink. This has inspired modern experiments testing various species in the crow family. Ravens understood the value of large rocks over small, understood the right number of stones, and so on. The most accomplished species—the New Caledonian Crow of the South Pacific—showed a level of understanding of this problem similar to that of a five- to seven-year-old human.

A raven solving the puzzle

Common Raven

It seems counterintuitive that so many birds in hot climates are black (a color that absorbs heat), but studies have found that the advantages outweigh the disadvantages. Dark feathers do get hotter than white feathers. But because feathers provide such good insulation, very little of that heat actually reaches the skin. In a light breeze, birds with black feathers actually stay cooler than white birds, because the dark feathers absorb light and heat at the surface, where it can easily radiate back to the air. White feathers allow light to penetrate into the feathers, closer to the skin, where heat is not so easily transferred back to the air. In addition, black feathers are more resistant to wear and help block UV radiation.

Every bird is covered with feathers. And almost every feather on a bird has a different, specialized length, shape, and structure to do exactly what is needed at its particular position. For example, feathers around the head all serve a role. There are tiny feathers around the eyes, bristles at the base of the bill, and longer feathers on the throat. Among the most specialized are the feathers that cover the ear opening. These must allow sound to pass through but also protect against debris and create a surface over the ear for air to flow across as smoothly and quietly as possible. The noise of air turbulence can reach 100 decibels in our ears at speeds as low as 25 miles per hour, the normal flight speed for most birds. That much noise makes it difficult to hear anything else and causes hearing damage in humans with long-term exposure. A smooth ear covering helps birds avoid both of those problems.

Some of the specialized feathers around the face; the ear covert feather, a small feather that covers the ear opening, is at the lower right.

103

JAYS

Flashing white in the wings and tail might help to startle a predator at the moment of attack.

A Blue Jay taking off with an acorn

■ This colorful bird visits birdfeeders throughout the East and is common in wooded areas, like suburbs and city parks. When theories of protective coloration were first being debated around 1900, birds like the Blue Jay were a puzzle. It was difficult to imagine how such flashy colors could help birds camouflage themselves! Now we know that color patterns evolve for many reasons, not just for camouflage. The head pattern of the Blue Jay is probably to disrupt the perceived shape of the head, making it confusing for a predator to recognize the bird or to tell what direction it is looking. The bright white flashes in wings and tail probably help by startling a predator in the moments before an attack. One experiment found that predators hesitated when their prey moved quickly—and even more so if the fast movement was accompanied by a sudden flash of color. So a panicked Blue Jay taking off in a burst of movement and flashes of white could cause a predator to flinch—which might allow the jay to escape.

■ Birds, including jays, can be loud. For example, if a rooster crowed in your ear, the sound would be as loud as if you were standing within two hundred feet of a jet engine. A bird's ear is less than an inch from its mouth. So how do they avoid damaging their own hearing when they call? A few ways: As the jaw opens, the external ear canal closes to shut out sound. Increased air pressure in the inner ear also helps dampen vibration. Birds also can restore damaged hearing by growing new hair cells inside their ear, something humans cannot do.

Steller's Jay calling

A Blue Jay sunning

■ When *sunning*, a bird spreads its wings and fluffs its feathers to bask in bright sunlight, especially on hot days. Afterward, they usually preen. One likely benefit of sunning is that bacteria are inhibited by sunlight. Other possible reasons include soaking up vitamin D and controlling feather lice.

■ Jays are sometimes seen knocking bits of light-colored paint off houses and eating the paint chips. They are seeking calcium, an ingredient in most paint. Calcium is especially important for female birds forming eggshells. This paint-chipping behavior is most common in northeastern North America, where natural calcium is scarce, partly because acid rain leaches calcium out of the soil. This behavior also occurs when it's snowing, covering any natural sources of calcium available.

A Steller's Jay eating paint chips

ACTIVITY

Notice jays munching at paint in your neighborhood? You can help them (and stop them from chipping paint) by offering crushed eggshells left over from breakfast, which are a better source of the calcium that birds need. It may seem surprising that eggshells from birds (chickens) would be eaten by other birds, but this is perfectly healthy and common!

SCRUB-JAYS

A frequent visitor to bird feeders; especially fond of peanuts

California Scrub-Jay

Jays are experts at hiding food they want to save for later. They usually hide food in the ground by digging a small hole, stuffing the food into it, then covering it with a leaf or small rock. Using their amazing navigational abilities and memory, they can keep track of thousands of these different hidden items. They retrieve insects within days, but long-lasting items like seeds can be left for months. If a jay thinks it was seen hiding food, it will return secretly a few minutes later to move the food to a new, better hiding place. This shows a high level of intelligence, including an awareness of the intentions of other jays.

A California Scrub-Jay about to hide an acorn

A recent study in California found that many bird species are already adapting to warming temperatures. Many have started nesting five to twelve days earlier than they did one hundred years ago. That may not sound like a huge difference, but it's significant: The change in timing matches the temperature shift over the hundred-year period. Birds are probably trying to a) avoid high summer temperatures and (b) synchronize with plant and insect cycles that have shifted earlier. Resident birds can sense when conditions are changing and adjust accordingly. Long-distance migrants face a harder challenge, though. They begin heading back from their winter territory when days grow longer, yet return to find that the timing of plant and insect cycles on their usual breeding grounds has changed with the local climate. Birds are adjusting their arrival times in response to these changes, but there is evidence that, so far, many species are not adjusting quickly enough to keep pace. Time will tell whether the mismatch increases, or whether birds can adapt.

California Scrub-Jays

Three species of chickadees
inspecting everything

CHICKADEES

Clockwise from top right: Black-capped
Chickadee (found in northern states and
Canada), Chestnut-backed Chickadee
(Pacific region), and Mountain Chickadee
(western mountains). Named for their
"chick-a-DEE-DEE-DEE" call, their scolding
"dee-dee-dee" calls announce the presence
of predators.

Chickadees are the busybodies of the forest, peeping into crevices, studying twigs and pine cones, and constantly chattering about it. Curious, bold, and social, chickadees are among the most popular and well-known birds wherever they are. When they aren't nesting, chickadees are social and travel in small groups. Other songbirds understand the chickadees' calls and will often join their groups. A migrating warbler that has just landed in an unfamiliar woodland will benefit from bumping into local chickadees. Following them as they move through the forest will be safe and lead to the best sources of food and water.

Black-capped Chickadees in action

Like many other birds (and unlike humans), chickadees can see ultraviolet light—a whole range of color beyond purple. Male and female chickadees look alike to us, and to our eyes, both have white cheeks. But they look quite different to each other because they can see that males have a much stronger ultraviolet reflection on their cheeks.

Chickadees frequently visit bird feeders (they especially like sunflower seeds) and are often the first to discover a new feeder. Still, more than half their diet year-round is animal prey. In winter, they hunt for tiny, dormant insects and spiders, including eggs and larvae, which are found in bark crevices, dead-leaf clusters, and twigs. In the summer, they mostly bring small caterpillars to their nestlings (they can collect over a thousand in a day), but for the first week or so after hatching, the adults make special efforts to seek out spiders to feed their young. Spiders provide the nutrient taurine, which is essential for brain development and other functions.

A Black-capped Chickadee bringing a caterpillar to a fledgling

Chickadees that live in areas with harsh weather plan ahead and store food for the winter. A single chickadee can store up to a thousand seeds in a day, or eighty thousand in a season. This strategy is called scatter hoarding because the birds simply tuck food away in any crevice where it will fit. Incredibly, the bird can remember where each item is stored, and some information about which ones are the best quality and which ones have been eaten already. The hippocampus—the part of the brain involved in spatial memory—is larger in birds that live in colder climates, where storing food is more important. In fact, it grows larger in the fall, when birds have to start remembering where they hid food, and then it shrinks again in the spring.

A Black-capped Chickadee hiding a seed

Titmice are closely related to chicka-dees. The four species of titmice in North America all have drab grayish color and short crests.

TITMICE

Oak Titmice

■ As early as the 1300s the name *titmose* was in use in England, by combining the Middle English words *tit* (meaning "small") and *mose* (meaning "small bird")—literally "small small bird." After a century or two, this became *titmouse*.

■ Confronted with seeds of four different sizes, you might expect this titmouse to grab the biggest one. But a larger seed is harder to carry, more visible to anyone watching, and will take longer to break up and consume. All this involves more effort and increases the risk of attack by thieves and predators. Small seeds usually offer less food value and might not be worth the effort—yet if a small seed has high fat content and a lot of calories, it could be the best choice. The ideal seed would have just the right balance of pros and cons. This many-layered decision-making is going on every time a titmouse visits a bird feeder. If they choose either a larger or a smaller seed, it is because they took time to consider the best choice for that particular moment.

A Tufted Titmouse faced with a decision

■ Titmice (and chickadees), unlike many other small birds, do not eat at the bird feeder. They carry the food away and eat it elsewhere. You will usually see them fly to a bird feeder, sort through the seeds there for a second or two, then select one and fly back into the woods to eat it or hide it. Once in the cover of woods, the titmouse holds the food item between its feet and uses its bill to pry it apart for eating.

A Tufted Titmouse flying away from the feeder after selecting a seed

■ Songbirds typically lay four or five eggs. Parents begin incubating after the last egg has been laid—which means the eggs all develop together and hatch around the same time. For the Tufted Titmouse, the incubation period averages thirteen days, while for the Eastern Phoebe, it's closer to sixteen days. Why have such differences evolved? A recent review suggests that one of the most important factors is sibling rivalry. A young bird gains a selfish advantage by hatching sooner than its nest-mates. This "race" to hatching leads to shorter incubation times. Still, the embryo needs enough time to develop fully so it will grow into a healthy adult.

Tufted Titmouse nestlings nearly ready to fledge

A pair of Bushtits building their nest

BUSHTIT

■ Bushtits are the smallest non-hummingbird birds in North America, slightly smaller than the Golden-crowned Kinglet. Five of them together weigh just one ounce. They are found in western states in open brush and gardens. They usually travel in flocks of up to several dozen, constantly flitting and chattering through the foliage of shrubs and trees. Though quite similar to Chickadees, they are not related.

■ Despite its tiny size, the Bushtit builds a very impressive nest—a woven hanging basket that is up to a foot long. All songbirds follow similar steps in nest-building: Create a foundation, add material to form the structure, and then finish the inside with a soft, insulating lining. All this is instinctive. Birds don't need to be taught how to build an intricate nest typical of their species—they just know. The Bushtit is one of the few species known to use two different styles of nest-building, depending on the setting and the time of year. So while nest-building is instinctive, it also allows for flexibility to adapt to different surroundings.

Step 1: The nest always begins with a ring of spiderwebs and fibers creating the rim.

Step 2: can go either one of two ways:

A: Create a flat platform of loosely woven material. The female then sits inside it to stretch the shape into a cup, weaving and adding material from the inside to fill any gaps. Then she keeps stretching and adding more material to form the long, hanging pouch.

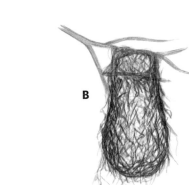

B: Quickly create a loosely woven pouch at nearly full size, then weave in material from both inside and outside to fill gaps and create a finished nest.

Nest type A is used more often early in the nesting season and in more open locations. It takes longer to build, but it is stronger. Nest type B is used more often later in the summer and in areas where there will be more places to hide and cover. It is made more quickly and is less sturdy.

In two to seven weeks, the nest is finished; the hood over the nest opening is built last.

■ One important function of nests is as insulation. Eggs and young nestlings must be kept at a constant temperature. They will die if they get too cold or too hot. Bushtit nests provide a lot of insulation. In one study in Arizona, the interior of nests in full sun reached only 84°F when outside the nest was over 111°F. The nest also keeps warm on cold nights. Because of this excellent insulation, Bushtit adults have to incubate their eggs only 40 percent of each day, allowing both members of a pair more time to forage.

Bushtit nest in cross section

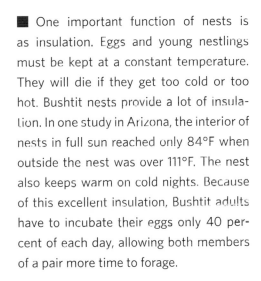
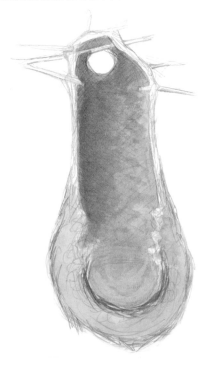

Nuthatches cling to tree bark with their sharp-clawed feet and can move in any direction across the trunk and branches.

White-breasted Nuthatch (upper) and Red-breasted Nuthatch (lower)

Both species of Nuthatches nest in tree cavities. The female builds a grassy nest inside the cavity. Red-breasted Nuthatches then "paint" the entrance hole with sap that they carry from pine, spruce, or fir trees, using either their bills or small bits of bark as paintbrushes. The sticky resin stops squirrels and other birds from entering the hole, yet, somehow, the nuthatches can dive through it without getting stuck! White-breasted Nuthatches have a similar behavior, sweeping or wiping the outside of the nest hole with bark strips, leaves, or crushed insects. It's likely these have a strong odor that masks the birds' smell and repels predators, but the true function is not known for certain.

White-breasted Nuthatch applying scent to the entrance to its nest

A White-breasted Nuthatch climbing

Nuthatches spend a lot of time clinging to the bark of trees, like woodpeckers, but the similarities end there. They do not chisel into wood with their bills; instead, they pick food from the bark. When visiting bird feeders, they quickly grab a seed and fly back into a tree. Wedging the seed into a crevice of bark, they pound it open with their bills. This is apparently the origin of their name—they are really nut hackers. White-breasted Nuthatches are resident, meaning they stay put and defend their territories year-round. But many Red-breasted Nuthatches nest in the far north, and in years when the numbers of spruce and pine seeds in the northern forests are low, they move south in huge numbers.

Female (top) and male (bottom) White-breasted Nuthatch

Male and female White-breasted Nuthatches are quite similar in every way. Usually the only way we can tell them apart is by the color of the crown. The male has a shiny black crown, while the female's is gray.

White-breasted Nuthatch threat display

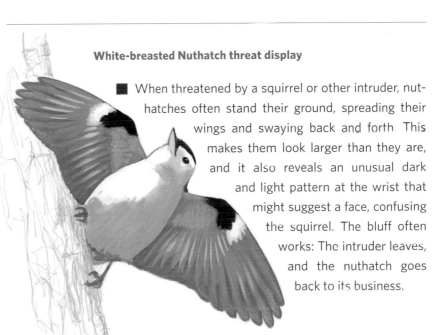

When threatened by a squirrel or other intruder, nuthatches often stand their ground, spreading their wings and swaying back and forth. This makes them look larger than they are, and it also reveals an unusual dark and light pattern at the wrist that might suggest a face, confusing the squirrel. The bluff often works: The intruder leaves, and the nuthatch goes back to its business.

WRENS

Most wren species are nonmigratory, and mainly eat insects.

A Carolina Wren singing

■ Among the most remarkable features of wrens are their iconic songs, which are loud, rich, and varied. Each male Carolina Wren knows up to fifty song phrases, which it performs to impress mates or rivals. Males from the western population of the Marsh Wren have an even more diverse repertoire of up to 220 songs!

■ Wrens dwell in shadowy thickets, creeping through tangled vines and tree stumps in search of insects and other invertebrates. Most species of wrens have a habit of keeping their tail raised up, flicking it or bouncing their whole body up and down when excited. These movements and postures allow birders to distinguish wrens from other small songbirds at a glance.

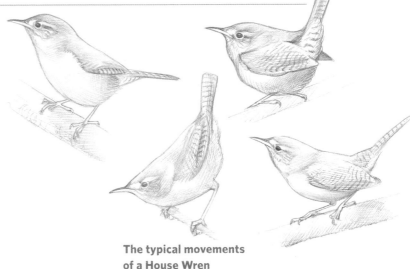

The typical movements of a House Wren

House Wren scolding

■ In the same way that kingbirds attack hawks, small songbirds will "mob" and harass a predator by calling loudly at them. Calls from one bird attract other birds. Soon enough, a small "mob" of many species gathers around, noisily chirping. Bolder birds will even swoop in to peck at the predator's back. This has two benefits: It annoys and distracts the predator, and it alerts all the other prey in the area that a predator is around. Most predators catch their prey by approaching them stealthily and surprising them. So letting predators know they have been seen takes away that advantage. Songbirds' most aggressive mobbing tactics come out during the breeding season and near their nests. In the fall and winter, a hawk, owl, or cat will be approached and scolded but not attacked.

Why don't we find dead birds?

Few birds die of old age. Unfortunately, many healthy birds are killed by predators or accidents. If a bird is old or sick, it is even more vulnerable. Birds usually don't die in a way that leaves their bodies on the ground where we might find them. And if a bird does die and fall to the ground, its body is usually scavenged quickly by another animal. The causes that most often lead to a human encounter with a dead bird are all human-related. For example, you might find a bird stunned or killed after flying into a glass window, or killed by house cats allowed outdoors, or dead along the roadside after being hit by a vehicle.

ACTIVITY

What's the best way to attract small birds? Try a birding technique known as "pishing." All you have to do is make a *"pshh-pshh-pshh"* sound, which mimics the call of a scolding wren or chickadee. This often works to lure these small birds into view.

A deceased Carolina Wren

KINGLETS

The Golden-crowned Kinglet is one of the smallest birds in North America, smaller than some hummingbirds. They weigh about as much as a nickel, yet still manage to survive winters as far north as Canada.

Three Golden-crowned Kinglets on a winter spruce tree

■ For Kinglets, most of the day—up to 85 percent of daylight hours—is devoted to searching for food. They eat insects, which in the winter means mainly insect eggs and larvae found on twigs and bark. During the cold season, they probably need at least eight calories a day, which may not sound like much. But if we ate at the same rate, a hundred-pound person would need about sixty-seven thousand calories, which is about twenty-six pounds of peanuts, or twenty-seven large pizzas, every day!

■ The circulatory system of birds is not so different from ours. Like us, they have a four-chambered heart that pumps blood through arteries and veins, which then carry fuel to the whole body and return waste products to be exhaled or excreted. There are differences in size and scale, though. A bird's heart is relatively large, compared with its body weight. And its heart beats much faster than ours. A bird as small as a Golden-crowned Kinglet has a resting heart rate of over six hundred beats per minute (ten per second), about ten times faster than the average human's.

A Golden-crowned Kinglet, showing the size and position of the heart

■ Small birds lose about 10 percent of their body weight each night while they sleep. Half of that is by excretion, and half is by burning fat and evaporating water. Imagine a hundred-pound human losing ten pounds overnight and gaining it back the next day! This overnight weight loss can be even higher on warm nights. On cold nights, birds become torpid, reduce their body temperature, and stay snuggled into their feathers, using them like a big sleeping bag. A bird can lose 30 percent of its body weight before suffering serious consequences. In those conditions, bird feeders can be a critical resource, allowing birds to refuel quickly and easily.

A sleeping Golden-crowned Kinglet

■ What do salmon have to do with kinglets? Everything is connected in nature! Salmon swim long distances upstream to spawn, where predators catch them and drop them in nearby forests. The fish bodies carry nutrients from the ocean onto land, fertilizing the soil. Studies show that spruce trees can grow three times faster along a stream with salmon than along a stream without salmon. More plant growth means more insects, and that means more insect-eating birds like Golden-crowned Kinglets. Salmon provide a dramatic example of this sort of nutrient transport, but it happens all around us all the time.

A Golden-crowned Kinglet hunts insects around the remains of a salmon.

119

AMERICAN ROBIN

An American Robin pulling a worm from the ground

■ The American Robin is one of the most familiar and beloved birds in North America. No matter where your backyard is—from Boston to Nebraska to California—if you have a grassy lawn, chances are you will see robins there hunting earthworms.

I thought robins were a sign of spring, but a flock just visited my yard in midwinter.

Robins depend on fruit in the winter, and like waxwings, their winter range is determined largely by the availability of food. The expansion of suburbs and the widespread cultivation of exotic fruit trees, with the recent spread of invasive berry-producing plants (like bittersweet and buckthorn) mean that robins can now find winter food much farther north (and a warming climate helps). Robins have benefitted from invasive species and human development of the landscape for at least two centuries. Their favorite summer food, the earthworm, was introduced to North America from Europe and thrives in lawns, and their primary winter food (fruit) is more common in the hedgerows and edge habitats we create.

American Robins eating sumac berries

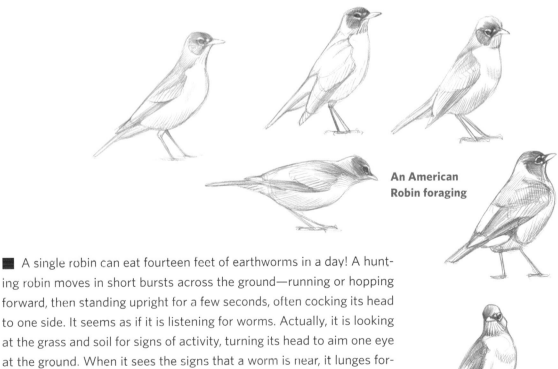

An American Robin foraging

■ A single robin can eat fourteen feet of earthworms in a day! A hunting robin moves in short bursts across the ground—running or hopping forward, then standing upright for a few seconds, often cocking its head to one side. It seems as if it is listening for worms. Actually, it is looking at the grass and soil for signs of activity, turning its head to aim one eye at the ground. When it sees the signs that a worm is near, it lunges forward, stabbing into the soil and gripping the worm in its bill. After a very brief tug-of-war (the robin almost always wins), the worm is pulled out and either swallowed whole or carried back to the nestlings.

The nesting cycle of an American Robin

After a pair selects a nest site, the female builds the nest (the male may help by bringing some nesting material to her). The nest begins with a foundation of strong twigs, then grasses stuck together with mud, ending with fine grass for the lining. Building can take four to seven days.

Three to four days after the nest is finished, the female lays the first egg. She will lay one a day until the clutch is complete at three to six eggs. The eggs of the American Robin are a beautiful greenish blue.

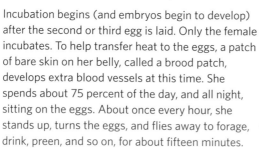

ACTIVITY

If a bird has built a nest by your front door, what should you do? If you move the nest, the adult birds will most likely abandon it. Try to give the birds as much privacy as you can. Use the door as little as possible and walk through calmly and quietly when you do. As days pass, the adult birds will become more accustomed to your presence. The whole nesting process will take only about four weeks, and it is fascinating to watch unfold—even from a distance.

Incubation begins (and embryos begin to develop) after the second or third egg is laid. Only the female incubates. To help transfer heat to the eggs, a patch of bare skin on her belly, called a brood patch, develops extra blood vessels at this time. She spends about 75 percent of the day, and all night, sitting on the eggs. About once every hour, she stands up, turns the eggs, and flies away to forage, drink, preen, and so on, for about fifteen minutes.

122

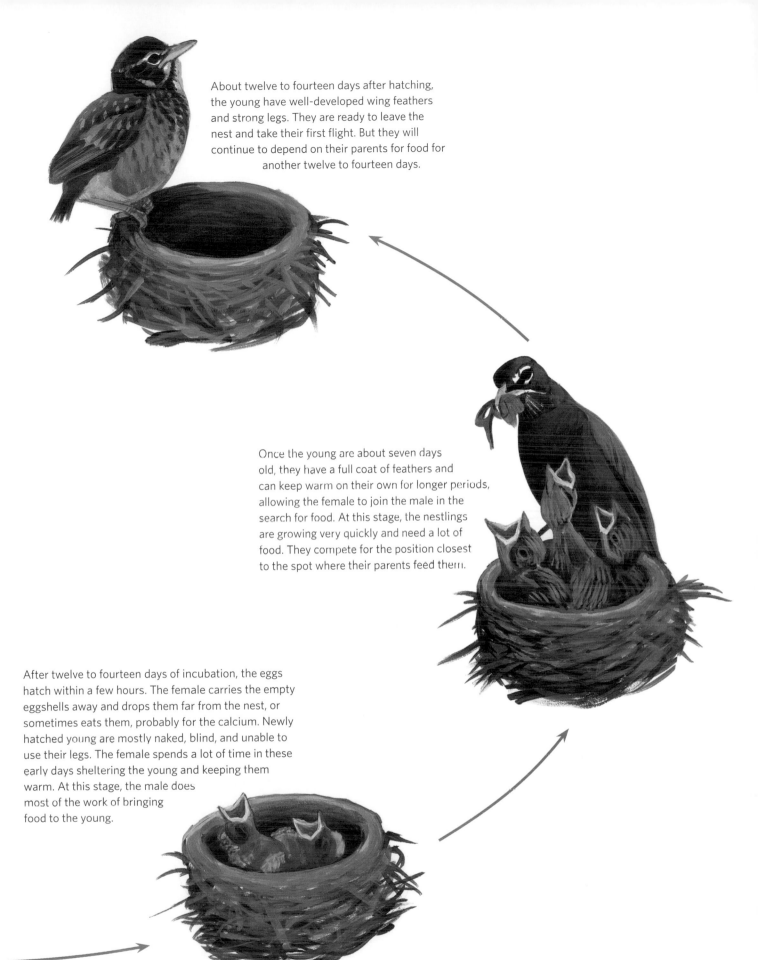

About twelve to fourteen days after hatching, the young have well-developed wing feathers and strong legs. They are ready to leave the nest and take their first flight. But they will continue to depend on their parents for food for another twelve to fourteen days.

Once the young are about seven days old, they have a full coat of feathers and can keep warm on their own for longer periods, allowing the female to join the male in the search for food. At this stage, the nestlings are growing very quickly and need a lot of food. They compete for the position closest to the spot where their parents feed them.

After twelve to fourteen days of incubation, the eggs hatch within a few hours. The female carries the empty eggshells away and drops them far from the nest, or sometimes eats them, probably for the calcium. Newly hatched young are mostly naked, blind, and unable to use their legs. The female spends a lot of time in these early days sheltering the young and keeping them warm. At this stage, the male does most of the work of bringing food to the young.

THRUSHES

Wood Thrush

The Wood Thrush is related to the American
Robin. Both sing extraordinary songs.

■ Wood Thrushes live in shaded forest. In summer, each pair defends a small nesting territory and returns to it each year. This is essentially a bit of private property to nest and raise young, and the nesting pair will defend their territory against others. Each Wood Thrush also defends a small territory on its wintering grounds in Central America. A Wood Thrush might spend its whole life on the same few acres each summer and winter, with a 1,500-mile commute in between.

■ Thrushes have unusually large eyes, an adaptation to their preferred habitat in the shady understory. Research has shown that eye size is linked to activity in low light, and birds with large eyes tend to start their day earlier and end it later. This could be one of the reasons that the melodious songs of thrushes are such a prominent part of the dawn and dusk chorus, before and after most other birds sing.

Hermit Thrush

■ For thousands of years, humans have enjoyed birdsongs, and the songs of thrushes in particular. Even among the thrushes, the Hermit Thrush is often singled out for praise. A recent study of Hermit Thrush songs found that they often use pitches that are mathematically related by simple ratios and follow the same harmonic series as human music. The harmonic series is a fact of physics, not a creation of human culture, so it makes sense that other vocal animals use it. In fact, this shows that the fundamentals of music are rooted in nature and have an instinctive appeal.

Hermit Thrush singing

syrinx

■ Birds produce sound with the syrinx. A syrinx differs from our larynx. It's made of two sets of tiny muscles that control airflow, allowing the birds to produce two sounds at the same time. In many songbirds, one side makes higher sounds while the other makes lower sounds. Notes from the two sides often match up seamlessly to sound like one note. In some cases, as in the songs of thrushes, the two sides produce entirely different notes simultaneously, creating an incredibly rich and complex sound. Simply put, the thrush can harmonize with itself.

A thrush, showing the position of the syrinx in the body

A male Eastern Bluebird investigating a potential nest site

Bluebird populations have increased greatly in the last fifty years, probably helped by human-made nest boxes.

BLUEBIRDS

■ With their gentle manner and pleasing colors, bluebirds are some of the most beloved birds in North America. They are classified in the thrush family, related to the American Robin and the Wood Thrush. They differ from other thrushes in their choice of habitat (open fields and orchards) and nesting site (in the cavity of a tree) and in their social habits (traveling in small groups of five to ten birds). They eat mainly insects and fruit, but in recent years some bluebirds have begun to frequent bird feeders, where they eat sunflower hearts, mealworms, and more.

■ There is no blue pigment in birds. All their blue color is produced by the microscopic structure in feathers. If you find a blue feather, you will notice that it is blue on only one side, and it actually looks drab brownish when light shines through it. The bluebird's color relies on the same physical principles as iridescent hummingbird feathers: A scattering of light boosts some wavelengths, while lessening others. The structure behind the color is quite different, though. Bluebirds' feathers have a spongy layer inside filled with tiny air pockets and channels. These air pockets are all about the same size. Together, they produce a patterned structure with intervals that perfectly match the wavelength of blue light. Waves of blue light scattered from one air pocket will be in phase with waves of blue light from some of the other air pockets. Light of other wavelengths will be out of phase and mostly invisible.

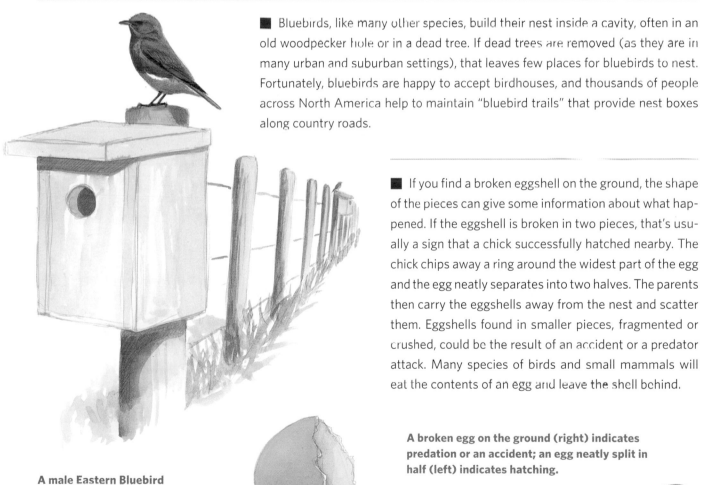

■ Bluebirds, like many other species, build their nest inside a cavity, often in an old woodpecker hole or in a dead tree. If dead trees are removed (as they are in many urban and suburban settings), that leaves few places for bluebirds to nest. Fortunately, bluebirds are happy to accept birdhouses, and thousands of people across North America help to maintain "bluebird trails" that provide nest boxes along country roads.

■ If you find a broken eggshell on the ground, the shape of the pieces can give some information about what happened. If the eggshell is broken in two pieces, that's usually a sign that a chick successfully hatched nearby. The chick chips away a ring around the widest part of the egg and the egg neatly separates into two halves. The parents then carry the eggshells away from the nest and scatter them. Eggshells found in smaller pieces, fragmented or crushed, could be the result of an accident or a predator attack. Many species of birds and small mammals will eat the contents of an egg and leave the shell behind.

A male Eastern Bluebird on a nest box

A broken egg on the ground (right) indicates predation or an accident; an egg neatly split in half (left) indicates hatching.

NORTHERN MOCKINGBIRD

A Northern Mockingbird singing

The mockingbird gets its name from its habit
of mimicking the songs of other species.

■ An individual Mockingbird can imitate over 150 sounds. They are not mocking the species they imitate, just showing off their own vocal talents. Copying sounds they hear is an easy way to expand their repertoire, and they can even mix them up every time they sing.

A Northern Mockingbird wing flashing to scare insects

■ You might notice a mockingbird standing on the lawn and flicking its wings open above its back. This is known as wing flashing. It's a trick birds use to try to startle and scare insects out of hiding. Have you ever played a "made you blink" type of game? By lifting its wings suddenly, the Northern Mockingbird is making insects "blink." If an insect moves, even slightly, it reveals its location and the bird can try to catch it.

A Northern Mockingbird in attack mode

A bird is attacking me every time I walk through my yard!

Many species do this to defend their nest, and mockingbirds are particularly aggressive. They see humans as potential predators. Their attacks are meant mostly to annoy you so you'll leave the area. This aggression peaks during the period when eggs and young are in the nest, which lasts about three to four weeks for most songbirds. Like crows, Northern Mockingbirds can recognize individual humans, and humans that have actually disturbed the nest will be singled out for more aggressive attacks than those who simply walk past.

■ One of the things mockingbirds are known for is singing loudly at night, which usually makes them unpopular with their human neighbors. Research on other species has shown that birds living in cities have increased their nighttime singing. This is likely a response to daytime noise. The birds take advantage of the quieter hours to sing their message without interruption.

A Northern Mockingbird singing at night

EUROPEAN STARLING

Starlings adapted to living around
humans long ago.

European Starlings
at their nest

■ Native to Europe, starlings were introduced in New York City in 1890. They multiplied quickly, becoming one of the most abundant birds on the continent. As their numbers increased, they took over the nesting cavities of native species—like the Eastern Bluebird and the Red-headed Woodpecker—contributing to the decline of those species. In North America, starlings are considered an invasive species, in other words a nonnative species that can damage the environment. But starlings mean no harm. The North American continent had been altered by other invasive species long before starlings arrived here. Earthworms are nonnative, for example, and they profoundly alter plant communities by changing the chemistry and structure of the soil. Most of the backyard and roadside plants we see every day were also introduced from elsewhere: dandelion, buckthorn, most honeysuckle, and others, as well as hundreds of species of insects, including the honeybee. And humans are, of course, the ultimate invasive species. Starling populations in the United States have declined dramatically since the 1960s, likely due to changes in farming practices, and their impact is now greatly reduced.

■ It is a common misconception that birds can't smell. In fact, all birds can smell, and generally at least as well as we do. Some species smell amazingly well—albatrosses can track an odor from twelve miles away on the ocean! Recent research on starlings and other songbirds has shown that they can use odor to distinguish the age and sex of other birds and distinguish family from strangers. Birds also recognize and avoid the smell of predatory mammals. Other studies have found that birds are attracted to the odors that plants release when insects attack them.

Starlings use their sense of smell to decorate their nest with aromatic plants or other pungent items (like cigarette butts), which help repel insect pests from the nest.

Do birds take baths to get clean?

Yes, baths help birds to remove dirt from their feathers. But baths also help to restore the shape of feathers. Like human hair (think bed head), feathers can be bent and misshapen. Simply wetting and drying the feathers restores their original shape. Birds always follow a bath with preening, putting all their feathers in their place. This ensures that birds can properly fly.

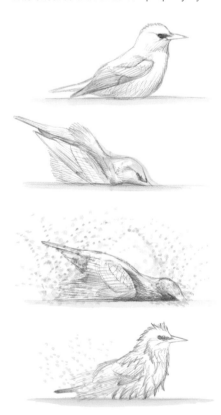

A European Starling bathing

A European Starling in winter colors (upper) and summer colors (lower)

■ The bill color of many species changes with the seasons. The European Starling's bill changes from yellow in the summer to blackish in the winter. The pigment melanin adds strength and increases the hardness of the bill for the cold months. Like many species, starlings shift from eating softer food like insects in the summer to harder food like seeds in the winter. A darker bill in the winter might be (at least partly) an adaptation to make the bill sturdy enough for crunchier, wintertime food. Melanin also strengthens feathers, and dark spots on eggshells serve to strengthen the shell and reduce the need for calcium, which is scarce.

WAXWINGS

Waxwings travel in flocks and wander the continent in search of fruit, their favorite food. They will stay in an area only as long as the fruit lasts, then wander again in search of the next meal.

Cedar Waxwings foraging for berries

■ Though waxwings have small bills, they open into unusually wide mouths, which allow them to swallow large pieces of fruit whole. Most North American songbirds nest in early summer—precisely the time when they can find plenty of food, like insect larvae on new plant growth. Waxwings also feed their young a protein-rich diet of insects, but they delay their nesting until later in the summer so their young fledge at a time when fruit is abundant.

A Cedar Waxwing swallowing a whole berry

■ Carotenoid compounds are common in fruits and seeds. Birds' bodies use these carotenoids to produce the range of red to yellow colors in their plumage. There are many carotenoids, and birds have evolved chemical processes to create the correct color from whatever food they are eating. An Asian honeysuckle however, provides a slightly different carotenoid that American birds are not used to and when they process this chemical it produces a deeper orange color instead of the typical yellow, and will stay that way until new feathers grow a year later.

A waxwing tail, showing orange tips, with one new feather replaced with the typical yellow tip

■ Filoplumes are a specialized kind of feather: tiny, slender plumes that grow in clusters around the base of other, larger feathers. The follicle where they enter the skin is packed with extremely sensitive nerve endings, which apparently allows a bird to sense the movements of individual feathers. Birds know when a feather is out of place, when two feathers are stuck together, when a fly has landed on a feather, etc. In flight, filoplumes allow birds to sense lift, drag, turbulence, updrafts, downdrafts, and other forces over their entire wings and body. The birds can use this information to make the tiny adjustments of wing and tail position necessary for flying efficiently.

Filoplumes growing next to a typical feather

WOOD WARBLERS

There are over fifty species of Wood Warblers in North America. Each is specialized for a certain habitat and can successfully build a nest and raise young only in that setting.

A male Black-throated Blue Warbler in mountain laurel

■ Scientists are still working to understand the remarkable details of the magnetic sense of birds. Birds can also detect polarized light, which helps them sense the position of the sun even when the sun itself is not visible. All these senses might be linked to the birds' vision, so it is possible that a songbird sees some sort of compass guide all the time. This information is essential for orientation during migration, but it could also be very useful for a bird navigating locally. Imagine seeing a compass reading all the time as you walked through your home or school. Birds could use this information as they navigate their own breeding territory, to help remember the locations of stored food, and more.

A Black-and-white Warbler with a totally hypothetical artist's rendering of what the bird might see in the sky: a blue band of polarized light and a reddish band oriented with the magnetic field, with a stronger dot showing the slope of the magnetic field

ACTIVITY

Imagine flying all night and landing in an unfamiliar place at dawn. Finding water, shelter, and food—all while avoiding predators—is a huge challenge! Even more so when much of the outdoors is covered with buildings, cars, lawns, and other human-made structures. In urban and suburban areas, small parks and gardens can be a magnet for migrating birds. You can make your yard, garden, or park bird-friendly by planting native shrubs and trees and offering water. The biggest benefit of using native plants for birds is that those plants have evolved over millennia to coexist with a whole ecosystem of insects and other organisms that birds like to eat. Exotic plants are not integrated with the local ecosystem, which means that fewer insects are able to use them. For example, in the eastern United States, native oak trees host more than five hundred species of moth and butterfly larvae. Meanwhile, non-native Norway Maples host fewer than ten species! For insectivorous birds, obviously, an oak tree is much more attractive. Furthermore, skip the insecticide, which can be very dangerous for birds. It's best to simply let the birds control the insects themselves.

A Black-throated Green Warbler foraging in a spring oak tree

■ The Black-throated Blue Warbler is typically found in moist, leafy understory, including under mountain laurel or rhododendron. Most other warbler species have particular preferences for habitat, and this makes them vulnerable as even small shifts in climate lead to changes in plant communities.

MORE WOOD WARBLERS

Blackpoll Warbler (top), Townsend's Warbler (center), and Hooded Warbler (bottom), showing some of the diverse color patterns of this group. The black pigment melanin is a key part of that variation.

Three species of wood warblers

Almost all the wood warblers are migratory, and the Blackpoll Warbler migrates the farthest distance of them all. Some nest in northwestern Alaska and winter in central Brazil. That's more than 7,000 miles away! In the fall, all Blackpoll Warblers gather along the northeastern coast—from Nova Scotia to New Jersey—to feed, rest, and build up fat reserves. Their tiny weight doubles before the flight, from 11 grams to over 23 grams. This fat is the fuel that will carry them on a 2,500-mile nonstop flight, in about seventy-two hours (three days straight), all the way over the Atlantic Ocean to the coast of northeastern South America. By the time they land, they will have lost all their extra weight. In the spring, they switch it up. Instead of one long journey back north, they travel in shorter hops, flying across the Caribbean to Cuba and Florida, then over land to their nesting territories. Birders in the North eagerly wait for their arrival each spring.

The annual migration cycle of the Blackpoll Warbler

Birds' bodies operate at very warm temperatures. Feathers insulate them, and their muscles generate lots of extra heat during activities like flying. So how do they cool down? One way is to pant. By opening their bills wide and expanding their throats to expose lots of moist skin, they can take in rapid puffs of air (triple their normal breathing rate) to evaporate water and cool the surfaces of their throats and air sacs. Ideally, they do this only when they have access to water to replenish what evaporates.

A female Common Yellowthroat panting

Why do birds sing?

Singing is a bird's way of announcing its presence and showing off for mates and rivals. Many species change their performance depending on who is around. For example, a male might use one song type to impress a female, another song type to intimidate rivals, and casual "practice" songs when it has no audience. Many singing performances also include a visual display, like flashes of bright color or acrobatic movements. A brightly colored throat is a feature shared by many species. When the bird sings, it raises its bill and its throat expands, making the color very noticeable, while in a normal posture, the color is less noticeable.

A male Common Yellowthroat singing and not singing

TANAGERS

Brightly colored tanagers are related to cardinals and live mainly in the forest canopy. This bird is molting from bright red summer plumage to greenish winter plumage.

A male Scarlet Tanager in the process of molting

■ Birds have evolved an excellent sense of time. Highly migratory species like Tanagers run on a strict schedule with the seasons. After they migrate in the spring, they immediately nest. Then, in the few weeks between nesting and fall migration, they molt all their feathers. Activities that take a lot of energy—like nesting, molting, or migrating—rarely overlap. Certain genes are associated with time cycles, which can allow birds to begin and end migration on time.

■ Tanagers give no thought to hopping from twig to twig eighty feet up in the air, then jumping into the open air to catch a passing insect. Can birds be afraid of heights? Some fear of heights is instinctive. Walking off a cliff would be bad, so most animals, including baby birds, instinctively avoid the edge. Once a bird can fly, though, the cliff doesn't seem so dangerous. They are comfortable balancing on the edge or even stepping off, knowing they can spread their wings and come right back.

A Western Tanager perched above the forest canopy

■ Preening is one of the most important chores a bird has to do. They preen for about 10 percent of each day! Some details of bills have evolved specifically for preening. A few species have specialized claws to clean and adjust their feathers and remove parasites. Birds also have a gland at the base of their tail that produces an oil used for feather care. Preening typically involves reaching back to this preen gland, getting a little oil on the bill, and then using the bill to tidy each body, wing, and tail feather from base to tip. This resets all the barbs and straightens the feather, while also spreading oil across it. A session of preening often ends with the bird leaning forward, raising all the feathers away from the body, and shaking like a wet dog, sending bits of dust floating away.

Typical preening motions

A Scarlet Tanager eating elderberries

■ Many birds eat fruit, and most fruit has adapted to be eaten and scattered by birds. Once swallowed, the fleshy part of the fruit is digested, and the hard seeds are either regurgitated or excreted, intact, usually within a few hours. In this way, birds scatter seeds widely across the landscape. One study found that birds migrating from Europe carry seeds to the Canary Islands, across several hundred miles of ocean.

CARDINALS

A male Northern Cardinal offering food to a female

In the breeding season (spring and summer), it is common to see an adult male cardinal feeding an adult female. The males show off their ability to find enough food to share with their mate.

■ Named for its bright red color, like the robes of the cardinals of the Roman Catholic Church, this is one of the most recognizable birds in North America. Cardinals thrive in the suburbs, surrounded by open lawns with trees, shrubs, and bird feeders. In 1950, they were found north only to Southern Illinois and New Jersey; now they are seen as far north as southern Canada.

■ The pointy, triangle-shaped crest at the top of a Northern Cardinal's head is all feathers. Birds with crests use them to communicate. They raise the feathers when they are excited or aggressive and lower them when they feel relaxed or nervous.

A Northern Cardinal with crest raised and lowered

A male Northern Cardinal singing

■ Birds are very sensitive to day length. Changes in day length trigger hormonal changes. Male cardinals sing from treetops beginning on the first sunny days after the winter solstice. This happens even when the air is still cold and the ground is covered with snow. Early human observers saw this brilliant red bird as a sign that spring was on the way. The bird was thought to be singing *"cheerily cheerily cheer, cheer, cheer, cheer."*

■ When it leaves the nest, a young Northern Cardinal has a dark bill. A few weeks later, the bill turns bright orange-red like that of adults. The feathers on these young birds are often flimsy, having grown quickly so they can fledge from the nest as soon as possible. More adultlike feathers will replace them within a few weeks, before the harsh winter weather sets in.

A young cardinal just a few days after leaving the nest

Related to cardinals, the grosbeaks are migratory species that nest across the United States and southern Canada and winter in Central America.

GROSBEAKS

A female Rose-breasted Grosbeak and fledglings

■ Why do birds migrate? After all, migrating has many downsides: It's dangerous, takes a lot of energy, and requires extreme adaptations. Even brain size is linked to migratory habits. Having a large brain takes a lot of energy—which makes it incompatible with long-distance flights. That means migratory species generally have smaller brains. About 19 percent of the world's bird species, billions of birds, migrate every year. They do it because the benefits (more food and less competition for territories) outweigh the risks. Would you travel farther to get to a grocery store that is less crowded, with better selection and lower prices? The trip is not easy, but the results are so good it's worth the extra distance.

■ Birds have an incredibly precise sense of body position. They can balance on a tiny twig, stand on one leg, and fly through strong wind. Birds have two balance sensors: One is in their head (in the inner ear, much like ours), and the other is in their pelvis. This means they can keep track of the movement of two body parts at the same time.

A Black-headed Grosbeak balancing on a twig with the help of an extra balance sensor in its pelvis

■ A large bill like a grosbeak's is designed for cracking seeds. The key to cracking hard seeds is strong jaw muscles. At bird feeders, these species enjoy sunflower seeds and are among the few birds that can crack and eat extra-crunchy safflower seeds. In the wild, their diet is 20 percent fruit, more than 50 percent insects, and 30 percent seeds. To open seeds, grosbeaks use the cutting edges at the sides of their bills, position the seed, and bite down to split it open, then they manipulate the shell and the seed with their tongues. Pieces of the shell are pushed away and dropped from the side of the bill, while the seed is saved.

A Rose-breasted Grosbeak, showing large bill and wide jaw

■ Birds have a third eyelid called the nictitating membrane to protect the eye. It's a thin, translucent or clear membrane that flicks across the eye, while still allowing some vision. It's rarely seen in real life because it moves so quickly. It is probably used a lot in flight to guard against oncoming insects, dust, and twigs, almost like goggles. Songbirds use it as they snap up insects while flying. Woodpeckers close it as their bills hit wood. This grosbeak is closing it to protect its eyes as the husk of a seed cracks.

A Rose-breasted Grosbeak with the nictitating membrane mostly closed

BUNTINGS

A male Lazuli Bunting (left), a male Indigo Bunting (right), and a female Indigo Bunting (below)

■ Related to cardinals and grosbeaks, buntings are small finch-like birds. Buntings are sexually dimorphic—the males and females look different and have different habits and roles. In most sedentary species (those that stay put and do not migrate), pairs remain together all year and usually share the work of defending territory and raising young, and in most of those species, males and females look alike. In migratory species (like buntings), sexual roles often differ, and males and females look different. Males arrive on the breeding grounds first and establish a territory. Females come a few days later and select a mate. The most attractive males are more likely to be chosen, which drives the evolution of more showy plumage. As the female works to raise a family, drab-colored plumage is an advantage. It provides better camouflage and is less costly to produce, leaving her with more energy for migrating and for producing eggs.

■ The bird respiratory system is very different from ours and much more efficient. Humans have flexible lungs that expand and contract with each breath. The lungs of a bird are rigid and do not expand and contract. A system of air sacs controls airflow, and fresh air passes through the lungs in one direction on both inhale and exhale, continuously supplying oxygen. It is thought that this breathing system evolved in dinosaurs more than 200 million years ago, at a time when the earth had only half as much oxygen as today, and birds now reap the benefit. Birds are essentially never out of breath. If you see a bird panting after exertion, it is because of overheating. In experiments, hummingbirds can still fly at an oxygen level equivalent to 43,000 feet elevation! That's 50 percent higher than Mount Everest.

The adult male Painted Bunting is an incredible rainbow of brilliant colors, one of the most colorful birds in the world. Females and young are a much plainer olive color.

The respiratory system of a bird: the air sacs occupy a large part of the body of a bird, and some air sacs extend into the larger bones (not shown).

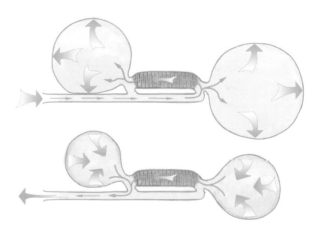

■ The Painted Bunting is found in the southeastern United States, from South Carolina to Texas. The population nesting along the Atlantic coast of the southeastern United States is unfortunately declining. One reason is the species' popularity as a cage bird, even though trapping and keeping native birds is illegal, a problem much more prevalent in Cuba than in the United States.

A greatly simplified schematic diagram of a bird's respiratory system, with air sacs in blue and lungs in purple. The air sacs expand to inhale (top) and contract to exhale (bottom), and fresh air always flows from back to front (right to left) through the lungs.

145

JUNCOS

These three are all regional variations of the same species. The three subspecies shown here are known as Slate-colored Junco (top, found mainly north and east), Oregon Junco (middle, found across the west), and Gray-headed Junco (bottom, found in the southern Rocky Mountains).

Three subspecies of Dark-eyed Junco

Most songbirds spend the summer as a pair on a territory, raising one or two broods of young, then go their separate ways migrating to the wintering grounds. In the case of juncos, females tend to migrate farther than males, and first-winter birds farther than older birds. At the southern edge of the winter range, you would see a higher percentage of immature females, and closer to the breeding grounds, more adult males. Many other species of songbirds do not segregate by age or sex, and each individual will return to the same small winter territory each year, in the same way that they are faithful to a summer territory.

Dark-eyed Juncos tending their nest

It's December—why are there almost no birds using my feeder?

The most likely answer is that they are finding plenty of natural food and simply don't need to supplement that with the bird feeder. Even if you are offering high-quality food in unlimited amounts, it probably requires some compromise or risk to reach it, like traveling across open areas. The birds may be more comfortable foraging all day in dense weedy thickets where they can stay hidden and find a diverse array of natural seeds and fruit, and even the occasional insect or snail. Once the winter weather closes in and natural food supplies dwindle, bird feeders become the best option for many birds and you should see a normal number of birds making the trek to your feeder.

Is a bird feeder just providing easy pickings for predators?

No. Studies show that predation at feeders is lower than in more natural settings. This is presumably because there are more birds watching for danger and sounding the alarm for any nearby threat. Feeders do pose a threat by indirectly increasing nest predation in the summer. Populations of crows, grackles, cowbirds, chipmunks, and others increase when they have access to feeders in the winter, and those species then go after nests in the spring. Some studies have found that species like cardinals and robins raise almost no young in neighborhoods with feeders.

Is my bird feeder making birds lazy?

No. Studies show that even birds that have lived with feeders for generations still get at least half of their food from the wild and use the artificial food only as a supplement. They suffer no ill effects when the feeders are removed. Feeders help them get through extreme winter weather when natural food is hard to find (such as an ice storm) but otherwise have little impact on survival.

Will feeding birds keep them from migrating?

No. The decision to migrate is based on many different factors, including date, weather, and the bird's body condition and fat reserves. If anything, it's possible that feeders might prompt birds to leave sooner, by making it easier to "fill the tank" before a long flight.

Migration requires a lot of information. Birds weigh many options before they decide to launch into the night sky to fly hundreds of miles.

A White-crowned Sparrow beginning a night of migration

■ Most small songbirds migrate at night, which makes their journeys even more remarkable and mysterious. The advantages of flying at night may include less turbulent air, cooler temperatures, fewer predators, and stars more visible for navigation. This way, daytime can be spent on refueling. After sunset, birds launch into flight, climb to several thousand feet, and fly for hours. How do they decide which night to fly? Their motivations are complex. In the big picture, changes in day length trigger hormones, which lead to physiological changes (meaning the way birds' function changes) that increase the bird's urge and ability to migrate. (Even pet birds in cages display this migratory restlessness in the spring and fall, including fidgeting and seeming active at night.) Each night, a bird might check its body condition, fat reserves, the current temperature, wind direction and speed, and more. It must consider all these factors before deciding to take off or to wait. Launching into the dark night is risky, but waiting might be even more risky.

■ Young birds are genetically predisposed—meaning it's in their genes—to learn the song of their own species and to ignore the songs of other species. They memorize song patterns they hear before they are three months old. Soon they begin to practice singing, controlling their voice until they can re-create the song model they memorized in their first few months. They will continue to sing this song for the rest of their lives.

A White-crowned Sparrow singing

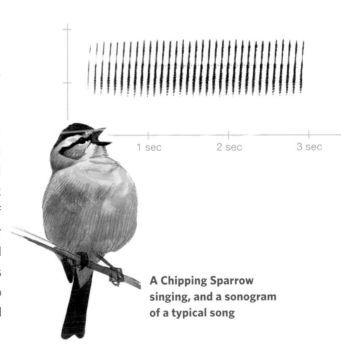

■ The song of a male Chipping Sparrow sounds like a simple trill: one note that is quickly repeated at the same pitch. This vocal performance depends on control and harmonization of the muscles in the two-part syrinx. Birds coordinate their breathing, bill position, and body movements to create a song that is just right. We could think of a bird's song as a kind of dance or gymnastics routine, a series of jumps, and the judges (potential mates and rivals) are looking for height and speed, along with precision and consistency. To us, they all sound pretty much alike, but birds have more sensitive hearing. Birds process sounds at least *two times* faster than we can. To get closer to what a bird hears, we would have to listen to a recording at half speed or slower.

A Chipping Sparrow singing, and a sonogram of a typical song

How do birds lay eggs?

One egg is a big process. The yolk builds up slowly. After a fertilized yolk is released, twenty-four hours pass before the egg is laid. It begins in the **oviduct**, where **albumin** (egg white) is added (in about four hours); then to the **uterus**, where the shell is formed (fifteen hours); and finally any coloration is added to the shell (five hours). A complete egg can be anywhere from about 2 percent to 12 percent of a female's body weight. The advantage of eggs is that the female can produce multiple eggs in a short time and deposit them in a nest. The embryos grow and develop in the nest while the mother can move around freely. If she carried four or five developing embryos and gave birth to live young, flight would not be possible during that time.

MORE SPARROWS

A Song Sparrow fighting with
its reflection in a window

Birds become extremely
territorial in the spring.
Within a few weeks, though,
their hormones calm down.

In the spring and early summer, many people find that a bird is attacking their windows or car side-view mirrors. The bird is not flying into the glass randomly or trying to get into the house—it is attacking its *own* reflection in the glass. The bird sees itself and, with breeding-season hormones making it more aggressive and territorial, confuses its reflection with a potential rival. This triggers the need to defend its territory and drive off the "intruder." Overall, this behavior is harmless (and is different from when birds collide accidentally into windows, which can be fatal).

ACTIVITY

If a bird attacks your bedroom windows (and even wakes you up), you can cover the outside of the glass so the bird won't see its reflection. The bird may just move to another window and continue its attacks there, though. The activity should taper off in a few weeks as the breeding season ends and the territorial drive fades.

Song Sparrows, from hot and dry Arizona (left) and cool and humid British Columbia (right)

From the Atlantic Ocean to the Pacific Ocean, and from Mexico to Alaska, the Song Sparrow shows a lot of variation in size, shape, and color. Birds living in more humid climates (like the Pacific Northwest) tend to be darker-colored than those in drier climates. The dark pigment melanin matches the surroundings (and so is better for camouflage) and also helps protect the feathers from bacteria, which are more common in humid climates. Another broad trend is that birds in hotter climates have relatively large bills and feet. Those parts of the body don't have feathers or insulation, so more heat escapes from them. In cold climates, the opposite is true: Smaller feet and bills help reduce heat loss.

As humans transform the landscape—with buildings, roads, and machinery—we also transform the soundscape. Our industrialized world is full of low-frequency noise. Since sound is so important to how birds communicate, any extra noise seriously affects them. Many species now avoid roads, industrial sites, and other noisy environments for this reason. Some species (such as the Mourning Dove, with its low-pitched song) simply avoid nesting in noisy places altogether. Birds that do live in noisy places shift the pitch of their songs higher, which helps to distinguish their sounds from low-pitched noise. Are birds' songs actually changing as a direct adaptation to communicate better through the noise? Or are birds simply trying to sing louder in noisy places and happen to produce higher-pitched sounds when they "shout"? It's not yet clear.

A Song Sparrow singing

151

OLD WORLD SPARROWS

The House Sparrow is one of the most successful and adaptable birds in the world.

House Sparrows thrive around people. Studies have traced this to the beginning of human agriculture in the Middle East, over ten thousand years ago. House Sparrows adapted by growing larger bills to take advantage of the grain being grown in large quantities by humans. As agriculture spread around the world, House Sparrows spread with it and continued to adapt. When House Sparrows were brought to North America in the mid-1800s, they had already spent ten thousand years adapting to humans. They quickly spread throughout the farms and cities of this continent. Before 1900, horse-drawn carriages and livestock were everywhere, and birds could eat any grain that was spilled. However, their populations have declined steadily over the last one hundred years, as farms and livestock have disappeared from large areas.

House Sparrows, showing the slightly larger bill and head of the human-adapted population (left)

A House Sparrow in flight, with all feathers outlined

How many feathers does a bird have?

Few attempts have been made to count all the feathers on a bird, but enough to make some general statements. Small songbirds like House Sparrows have about 1,800 feathers in the summer:

> About 400 on the head
> 600 on the underside of the body
> 300 on top of the body
> 400 on the wings (200 on each wing, mostly small coverts at the leading edge)
> 100 on the legs
> 12 in the tail.

Songbirds in cold climates have more feathers in the winter—about 2,400 total—adding about 600 small, downy feathers on the body. Larger land birds like crows have a few more feathers than small birds, but mostly they just have larger feathers. Waterbirds have a lot more feathers, particularly on the parts that are in contact with water.

Dust bathing is a common behavior in certain species, including the House Sparrow. You might find small, bowl-shaped dips in the ground where House Sparrows take dust baths. Just as in a water bath, birds crouch into the dust and shake their wings to move dust up and over the body. The reason for dust baths is unknown, but one hypothesis is that the dust helps control their preen oil. The right amount of preen oil helps waterproof and condition the feathers, prevents bacteria, and so on. But too much oil could cause feather barbs to stick together, provide food for bacteria and parasites, and more. Dusting may control oil levels.

A female House Sparrow dust bathing

Almost all songbirds fly on an undulating, wavy path, alternating between short bursts of wingbeats and brief glides.

FINCHES

A male and female House Finch building their nest

■ If you have small finches nesting on a windowsill, porch ledge, hanging plant, or Christmas wreath, they are undoubtedly House Finches. These small birds are regular visitors to bird feeders and—as their name suggests—houses. Adult males are bright red on the head and breast, while females are brownish and streaked, without red.

A typical male House Finch with red color (left) and one with yellow instead

■ All red, orange, and yellow color in songbirds comes from carotenoid pigments, which come from their diet. These compounds create the red and yellow colors found in many fruits and vegetables (like carrots and oranges), the colors of fall leaves, and much more. Birds' systems then modify the carotenoid molecules to produce a shade of red, orange, or yellow color. Carotenoids are also essential for the immune system. If a bird is sick when it is growing new feathers, it's possible that its feathers may look less vibrant. That's because it needs carotenoids to fight the disease and can't spare much for feather color. In House Finches, though, males range from bright red to yellow, and the link between color and health is unclear. The percentage of yellow males varies regionally—there are more in the Southwest and many in Hawaii—and the color probably has more to do with the specific carotenoids available and how they were processed and less to do with health.

ACTIVITY

Help keep birds healthy! Making sure your bird feeders and the areas around them are clean is one important way to reduce the chance of disease. If you do see any birds at your feeder with conjunctivitis, it is recommended to take all the feeders down and clean them with bleach, wearing gloves for safety. Rake away any seeds and droppings that have been left underneath the feeders. This bird feeder housekeeping is good to do regularly, even if you don't see any signs of disease.

A male House Finch with conjunctivitis

■ Even a minor illness is a very serious risk to birds. It makes a bird slower and less alert, and therefore much more vulnerable to predators. One disease sometimes seen at bird feeders is an eye infection called conjunctivitis. This is highly contagious and spreads through close contact, such as at bird feeders. An epidemic of conjunctivitis spread across the eastern United States in the mid-1990s, affecting mainly House Finches. The disease is still present but is less frequent now.

GOLDFINCHES

**Male (lower) and female (upper)
Lesser Goldfinches**

Goldfinches travel in flocks, and there
is some evidence that groups can stay
together for years over great distances.
They are frequent visitors to bird feeders,
and a flock will often sit calmly for minutes
at a time, perching and nibbling seeds.

A male American Goldfinch in drab winter plumage (right) and bright yellow summer plumage (left)

■ All birds molt. Many birds molt once a year and simply replace their old feathers with a similar-looking set. Other species—such as the American Goldfinch—molt twice a year and change their appearance dramatically with the seasons. This takes a lot of time and energy, so goldfinches (like many other species) molt all their body and wing feathers in the late summer, when life is more low-key. During this season, they can expect mild weather and plenty of food, and molting fits in between nesting and migration. In late summer, the goldfinch grows drab feathers that help camouflage it through the winter. Six months later, in early spring before nesting begins, goldfinches molt all their body feathers again (but not the wing or tail feathers). Males transform into the showy yellow and black colors they need for courtship. How can the same feather follicle grow different-colored feathers at different times? Hormones make this possible.

The body feathers of a male American Goldfinch, with a ray of light penetrating several layers and reflecting off each one

■ Goldfinches are among the most conspicuous bright yellow birds. There is a secret to the brilliant, glowing color of a male goldfinch. A single feather does not reflect enough light to be very impressive (in fact, each feather is thin and translucent, so most light goes right through it). Here's how goldfinch feathers work altogether, though, to glow: Each one is bright yellow at the tip (the part that is exposed) and bright white at the base. Feathers are arranged so that some of the yellow tips overlap. Some light reflects off the yellow surface of each feather, while other light passes through and is reflected back out by the bright white of the feather bases. The feathers of a goldfinch essentially form a translucent yellow film with backlighting.

BOBOLINKS AND MEADOWLARKS

The Bobolink and the Meadowlark
are related to blackbirds and
orioles. The songs of these birds
are some of the most iconic sounds
of summer hayfields.

Male Bobolinks singing

■ Male Bobolinks display by singing in flight. Flying requires steady breathing, while singing involves complex breath control. If we try to run and sing at the same time, we end up gasping for air. So how do birds balance these two activities? (And the song of the Bobolink is beautiful and impressive: It can be over ten seconds long with more than one hundred phrases.) For one thing, birds' lungs are much more efficient than ours. When we fill our lungs with air, the oxygen is rapidly absorbed. We can exhale to sing, but we won't get more oxygen until we inhale fresh air. A bird, on the other hand, can store fresh air in its air sacs so that while it is exhaling, its lungs are receiving fresh oxygen. Even with these adaptations, singing in flight is still a remarkable feat!

A male Bobolink singing in flight

■ To nest, these birds require a large open field with tall grass and little disturbance (for example, somewhere with no joggers or dog walkers). Fields meeting those requirements have become scarce in many areas—and so Bobolinks and meadowlarks have themselves become scarce. They are still common in the Great Plains and other areas with large hayfields. When they leave the breeding grounds, Bobolinks migrate in flocks to the grasslands of southern South America—one of the longest migrations of any songbird.

■ Birds and farming have always had a complicated relationship. Farmers blame birds for damaging crops. Yet they also appreciate the insect control that birds offer—birds eat more than 500 million tons of insects a year worldwide. Small family farms provide bird habitat in hedgerows, weedy edges, pastures, and other sites. In the early 1900s, much of the eastern United States was farmland. Species like the Eastern Meadowlark and Bobolink thrived, nesting on the ground in the open meadows and hayfields. But now, with small farming declining in many areas—and the land converted to less diverse large factory farms, forests, or buildings—most of this habitat is gone.

A meadowlark singing in a hayfield

An Eastern Meadowlark, showing the line of sight with bill open and closed

■ Meadowlarks' sharpest vision is focused slightly above horizontal. Since they spend most of their time on the ground, this may be an adaptation for looking up for danger. Their vision also faces forward, ahead of them, so they can see the tip of their bills (most birds can't). But this creates a larger blind spot behind the head, which means they have to turn their heads to see their surroundings more than most birds.

ORIOLES

A pair of Baltimore Orioles at their nest

Recent research suggests that many tropical species like orioles may have evolved from migratory ancestors.

■ Most oriole species reside in Central and South America, though several species migrate north to breed in North America. Migratory habits can adapt quickly. It has long been thought that migratory behavior is a more recent trait in birds, as sedentary tropical ancestors began increasing their seasonal trips north. A recent study suggests that migratory behavior actually appeared and disappeared over time as different species evolved and that many songbirds now living in the American tropics evolved from migratory species.

■ The shape of birds' eggs depends on the species and can vary from round to more elongated. The non-round, elongated eggs can be either asymmetrical (pointed at one end) or evenly symmetrical. There are many possible explanations for this variation. A recent study found a surprising link between egg shape and flight habits. Species that spend more time flying, or are stronger fliers, tend to lay eggs that are less round. This may suggest that egg shape has evolved, in part, in response to the requirements of flight. Perhaps as birds' bodies evolved to be light and streamlined for efficient flight, round eggs no longer fit, whereas narrower, elongated eggs could.

The Song Sparrow flies less and lays less pointy eggs (left) than the Baltimore Oriole (right).

Life Span and Mating

How long do birds live?

Most individuals live less than just one year! If they make it to their first breeding season, songbirds generally have about a 50 percent chance of surviving each year. Given the 50-50 odds, about one songbird out of a thousand would make it to ten years. Records show that the oldest Baltimore Oriole known was twelve years old, and the oldest songbird was an American Robin, at just under fourteen years. Larger birds generally live longer. For example, a Bald Eagle reached thirty-eight years. And seabirds are particularly long-lived, with one Laysan Albatross at least sixty-seven years old and counting. These are remarkably long life spans compared with similar-size mammals!

Do birds mate for life?

In songbirds, the answer is "Yes, but . . ." In a Baltimore Oriole pair, if both survive the winter, they will most likely find their way back to the same territory, recognize each other, and make another nesting attempt together. But the male and female each have a 50 percent chance of surviving the year, leaving only a 25 percent chance that both will make it back. So, yes, they generally mate for life—but in most cases, that lasts only for a single breeding season.

100 eggs laid

60 chicks
survive to
fledging

20 fledglings
reach the
wintering
grounds

Fall
migration

15 birds
return
to breed

First
winter

Spring
migration

15 One year olds
only half survive to breed again the following year

15 One year olds

8 Two year olds

8 Two year olds

4 Three year olds

4 Three year olds

2 Four year olds

2 Four year olds

1 Five year old

1 Five year old

May **Jun** Jul Aug Sep Oct Nov Dec Jan Feb Mar Apr May **Jun** Jul Aug Sep Oct N.

Year 1   **Year 2**

A population graph of Baltimore Orioles

COWBIRDS

Brown-headed Cowbirds have an unusual nesting strategy: They don't build nests or raise young.

A male Common Yellowthroat raising a Brown-headed Cowbird fledgling

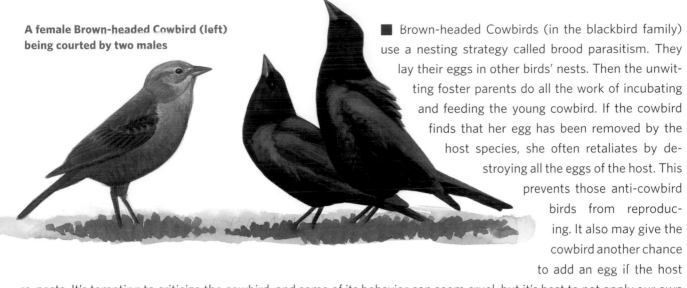

A female Brown-headed Cowbird (left) being courted by two males

■ Brown-headed Cowbirds (in the blackbird family) use a nesting strategy called brood parasitism. They lay their eggs in other birds' nests. Then the unwitting foster parents do all the work of incubating and feeding the young cowbird. If the cowbird finds that her egg has been removed by the host species, she often retaliates by destroying all the eggs of the host. This prevents those anti-cowbird birds from reproducing. It also may give the cowbird another chance to add an egg if the host re-nests. It's tempting to criticize the cowbird, and some of its behavior can seem cruel, but it's best to not apply our own values on the natural world. After all, humans and birds are not the same, and we live in totally different circumstances! The cowbird does not choose to lay her eggs in the nests of other birds—that's just the way cowbirds have evolved, and she seeks every advantage for her own offspring. It's a remarkable system, and for the cowbirds, it works extremely well.

■ The female searches her territory carefully for nests of other species where she can lay an egg. She lays one egg in each suitable nest, and can lay dozens of eggs in a season. Most egg-laying occurs in the morning, and in the afternoon, the cowbirds relax. Female cowbirds do not simply lay an egg and leave it. Research suggests that female cowbirds stay in their territory long after their young have hatched, to monitor the progress of the egg and the young, and that baby cowbirds as young as six days old respond to the rattle call of adult female cowbirds. After all, baby cowbirds have to avoid imprinting on, or forming an attachment to, their foster parents. The rattle call of the female cowbird from afar may be like a kind of instinctive password that helps baby cowbirds recognize their own species after they fledge.

A female Brown-headed Cowbird at a nest

■ Cowbird eggs hatch faster than those of other species, so as long as a cowbird egg is added to a clutch before incubation has started, it will hatch before the host's eggs. The young cowbird either pushes the unhatched eggs out of the nest or, being larger and stronger, simply gets to the food before other chicks can.

A Common Yellowthroat nest with one (larger and more densely spotted) Brown-headed Cowbird egg

163

GRACKLES

Like several other species, grackles benefit from human agriculture, with grain and other crops allowing grackle populations to grow.

A male Common Grackle displaying

■ The Common Grackle lives in suburban and rural habitats across the eastern two-thirds of the continent. They are large and strong and can prey on the eggs and young of smaller songbirds. Like crows and Brown-headed Cowbirds, grackles feed on corn and other crops, and are essentially fed by human agriculture. This allows their population to increase, which greatly affects the species they prey on. It's not their fault and doesn't have to detract from their beauty and splendor.

■ Some birds, including grackles and blackbirds, form large flocks that travel and roost together. Flocking, like colonial nesting, is common in birds that eat foods found in clusters. For species such as grackles, grain (their favorite food) is a challenge to find, but once found, there is plenty of it for all. Plus, when flocking, there are many eyes to watch out for predators or sound an alarm. Flocking is not an advantage when food is scarce and scattered. Chickadees, warblers, and similar species are more solitary or form loose groups. They search for food that is widely and sparsely distributed, such as insects or seeds, and they don't want other birds nearby to compete for the same piece of food.

A large flock of Common Grackles

**Common Grackles
with three kinds of
partial albinism**

■ Rarely, you may see a bird with patches of white in its plumage, or even entirely white or pale tan. These are all forms of albinism, which is the result of a lack of the dark pigment melanin. This happens in all bird species and can have many different causes: genetic mutations, illness, low nutrition, or injury. In some cases, the condition is temporary, and the bird will grow colored feathers in its next molt. In other cases, it is permanent. A complete albino has no melanin pigment, with entirely white feathers, and pink eyes and skin. Melanin is not just for coloration; it is also critical to vision and other bodily functions, so complete albino birds with no melanin at all, sadly, do not survive long.

■ What's up with birds' white and black droppings? Metabolizing, or processing, proteins creates a lot of nitrogen compounds, which need to be eliminated from the body because they can be toxic (ammonia, for example). Humans and other mammals convert these nitrogen compounds to less toxic urea, which is diluted with lots of water and stored in a bladder before being excreted from the body as urine. Birds can't afford to use that much water or carry that much weight, so they convert the nitrogen into a chalky substance, uric acid. This forms the white part of each dropping, while the dark part is undigested material that has passed through the intestines.

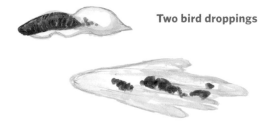

Two bird droppings

Wherever there is water and dense reeds or brush, you can find the Red-winged Blackbird. In larger marshes, hundreds nest in close proximity.

BLACKBIRDS

A male Red-winged Blackbird in full song display

One of the signs of spring, male Blackbirds return and start advertising on their territories as early as the first warm days in February. A male Red-winged Blackbird can choose to either hide or display its red shoulders. When a blackbird is relaxed, the wings are folded tightly against the body. Black feathers from the back and the breast wrap around, covering the red shoulder almost entirely. When the black body feathers are pulled back, though, the red shoulder is exposed. The male's full song display involves spreading the wings out from the body, fluffing up the shoulder feathers to make the red patches larger and more visible, and singing to draw attention to its display.

A Red-winged Blackbird with the red wing patch concealed by black body feathers (left) and exposed (right)

Sometimes when you look very closely at a feather in the right light, you can see faint bars across it, alternating light and dark. These are growth bars. They're similar to tree rings, but instead of a year, each dark-light combination represents a single twenty-four-hour period of growth. Darker bands grow during the day, and lighter bands at night. The rate of growth is generally only about a tenth of an inch a day, depending on the species and the bird's health and nutrition. This Red-winged Blackbird tail feather grew in about twenty days. Smaller species like wrens can grow their largest feathers in under ten days. Species like eagles and pelicans have much larger feathers, but those feathers still grow only a few millimeters a day, meaning that a single wing feather might take over one hundred days to grow.

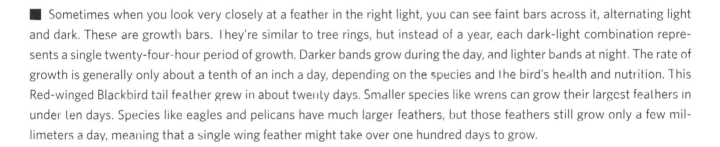

A tail feather of a Red-winged Blackbird, all black but showing the subtle shadings of growth bars

Millions of people feed hundreds of millions of pounds of birdseed to birds every year. All that bird food has to be grown somewhere. The challenge for farmers is to grow a crop that is tasty to birds, while also preventing wild birds from eating it in the fields before it is harvested and sold. Breeders have developed sunflower plants that are shorter (providing less foliage for birds to hide in) and have flowers that droop to face the ground (making them less visible and harder for birds to reach). Fields farther from wetlands are less vulnerable to blackbird attack, and various techniques are used to keep birds away from the fields.

Blackbirds flying over a field of bird food

What to do if . . .

A BIRD HITS A WINDOW

If a bird is stunned by hitting a window, pick it up gently and place it in a small cardboard box or a paper bag. Make sure the box or bag is closed and secured, with enough room for the bird to move around inside. Put it in a quiet, warm place where the bird can rest in the dark. Many birds will recover within an hour. Don't open the box/bag inside the house, not even for a peek!

If you hear scratching and fluttering noises inside the box/bag, this indicates that the bird is probably ready to go. Carry the box outside and open it up—hopefully, the bird will fly right out. If it doesn't, then leave it a while longer in the dark. There is no immediate need for food or water, so the bird will be fine for several hours. If the bird needs more care, you should look for a licensed wildlife rehabilitator in your area. If it doesn't recover, please see the below section, "You Find a Dead Bird."

A BIRD IS FLYING REPEATEDLY AGAINST A WINDOW

This is different from window collisions and is generally harmless. Birds sometimes see their own reflection as a potential rival and try to drive off the "intruder." Refer to page 151 (More Sparrows) for additional information.

A WOODPECKER IS ATTACKING YOUR HOUSE

First, figure out what the woodpecker is doing. Is it foraging for food? If so, you might need to call an expert to find out if you have insects in your walls. Is it just drumming? This behavior should taper off after a few weeks. In the meantime, you can try hanging something to discourage the woodpecker: a cloth or tarp to prevent it from reaching the wood, or strips of tinfoil to scare it off. Woodpeckers usually attack houses with natural wood panels, and one solution in extreme cases is to paint the house a different color.

A BIRD HAS BUILT A NEST ON YOUR PORCH

A few species of birds will nest on a porch, windowsill, etc. Give the birds as much privacy as you can and enjoy the opportunity to watch an entire nesting cycle!

A LIVE BIRD IS IN YOUR HOUSE

A bird inside a building will look for an exit and fly toward daylight, fluttering against (or crashing into) windows. It might fly close to you, but you are not in any danger. The bird is not attacking you, only looking for the way back outside.

Move slowly and calmly to avoid startling the bird. First close doors to keep the bird in the room it's in and stop it from entering other parts of the house. Then open all the windows and doors in that room to give the bird an easy exit. Close the curtains on any windows that can't be opened, leaving daylight only in the open windows and doors.

If you approach the bird, it will probably fly. Try to approach in a way that will "herd" it toward an exit without blocking its escape. Making yourself larger by spreading your arms above your head will help to prevent the bird from flying past you. Try to do this, like everything else, slowly and calmly. If the bird is fluttering against a window and you can pick it up, hold it gently but firmly and move immediately to an opening to let it outside.

YOU FIND A DEAD BIRD

Dead birds are most often seen as the result of a human-related cause. They may have collided with a window of a building, been hit by a car, or been killed by a pet cat. They may have gotten lead poisoning from ingesting lead bullets or fishing weights (if you know any hunters or fishers, encourage them to use nonlead materials.) It's unlikely that any dead bird you find is diseased, but handle it carefully and wash your hands.

The law: It is generally illegal to possess a native bird or any parts, such as feathers, without the proper permits.

In most cases, you should simply dispose of the body: Bury it or put it in the trash. If you know that a museum or university is interested in the bird as a specimen for study, follow these steps: Roll it carefully into a dry paper towel or a sheet of newspaper. Wrap that tightly in a plastic bag and be sure to include a note about where, when, and how you found the bird. Put it in the freezer until you can take the bird over. Wash your hands.

YOU FIND A BABY BIRD

Two key points before going any further:

- ▶ Most baby birds do not need any help! The best thing you can do is leave them alone, almost every time.
- ▶ Wild birds do not make good pets. More important, though, it is illegal to keep native birds. Only specially trained and licensed wildlife rehabilitators are allowed to keep injured or orphaned birds.

Assess the situation

If the baby bird looks something like this:

This is a fledgling. It is normal for birds this age to leave the nest. The parents are probably nearby, and the young bird should be left alone. If you hear a sharp, repeated call while you are close to the baby bird, or see an adult bird flying close to you, that is likely to be a parent defending its young. All you have to do now is move away and let them take over. Even if you do not see the parent nearby, do not put food and water near the fledgling. It might attract predators, and it won't actually help the bird.

Only a few situations will benefit from your intervention:

- ▶ *If a fledgling is in immediate danger* from cats, dogs, cars, etc. If you are convinced that it is in danger, simply shoo it toward safety, or gently pick it up and move it into a safer location, such as a shrub or tree.
- ▶ *If a fledgling is clearly injured* (for example, if it has been brought to you by a cat or dog). If the injuries are minor and the bird can sit and hop, it probably has its best chance in the wild with its parents. Set it on a high, hidden perch in a bush or small tree where the parents may find it. If its injuries are more severe, call your local wildlife rehabilitator.
- ▶ *If a fledgling is lost or orphaned.* It is unlikely that you will find an orphaned bird. The parents are probably close by, but it's still good to double-check. If you can, watch from a distance so as not to keep the parents away (for example, from inside your house), and watch constantly for a couple of hours. The parents will be stealthy when they visit, and it takes only a few seconds to deliver food to a fledgling. If you are certain the young bird is an orphan, call your local wildlife rehabilitator.

If the baby bird looks more like this:

This is a very young bird (unable to sit up) that has fallen from its nest. If you can find and reach the nest, put the baby bird back. If you can't find a nest or can't put the bird back, try to make a substitute nest and place it as close to the old nest as you can. A small box or bowl (e.g. a berry basket) lined with a paper towel should do the trick. Put the baby bird in it and watch from a distance to see if the parents return.

If, after all that, you are sure a baby bird needs your help, keep it warm and dry and call your local wildlife rehabilitator.

Becoming a birder

To get started in birding, all you need is curiosity! A bird identification guide and a pair of binoculars are considered the basic requirements, though many people now start birding with a camera instead of binoculars. As your birding hobby grows, these items will become essential. You can also find information and helpful discussion groups online.

Checking out local parks is a great place to start, especially early in the morning. And remember, birds' behavior is highly seasonal, so you may see totally different things at different times of year. Some parks offer bird-watching tours. And consider joining a local Audubon or nature society. You might be surprised to find that there are more birders in your neighborhood than you ever knew.

One good birding habit for all birds is to try to limit our effect on birds' behavior. Owls are especially sensitive to disturbance, but we should try to disturb all birds as little as possible. Watching from afar is the way to go (that's where the binoculars and camera zoom come in handy).

You will learn faster if you can be an active observer. Draw sketches, take notes, write poetry, take photos, try whistling some birdsongs—whatever will make you look and listen a little more carefully and a little longer.

One of the best approaches is to ask yourself questions. Here are some suggestions to get you started:

▶ What is the bird doing? How would you describe its movements? Is it interacting with other birds?

▶ What color is the bird? Does it have any contrasting color patterns? If so, what part of the bird is involved? Can you describe or sketch the color pattern you see?

▶ Do you hear any bird sounds? Are any other birds responding? Try to describe the sounds. How would you spell out the birds' song in letters?

▶ What is the bird eating? How does it move while it eats?

▶ What size are the birds you are seeing? How do they compare with one another?

▶ Study the size and shape of the bill. How does it compare with that of other birds around it? What would that particular bill shape be useful for?

▶ If you see a flying bird, notice how it flies. Is it following a straight path through the air or weaving, circling, or undulating? Is it in a flock or alone? Is it flying high in the sky or close to the ground?

The more you notice, the more you will learn!

Acknowledgments

This book relies heavily on the constantly growing body of published scientific research, and it would not have been possible without the curiosity and dedication of all of the people who work to advance our knowledge of birds and the natural world. Some of those people are listed as authors of the papers in the Sources section. Many thousands of others have also contributed to our current understanding of birds through those studies and countless more. I owe thanks to them all.

Thanks to the following people who helped directly with this book by answering questions, providing references, reading drafts, etc: Kate Davis, Lorna Gibson, Jerry Liguori, Klara Nordern, Danny Price, Jeff Podos, Richard Prum, Peter Pyle, J. Michael Reed, Marj Rines, Margaret Rubega, Mary Stoddard, Luke Tyrrell, and Joan Walsh.

Special thanks to these three people who put in extra time with research help, reading, rereading, and general consulting at various stages of the project: Chris Elphick, Lindall Kidd, and Tooey Rogers.

Thanks to my agent, Russell Galen, for being excellent at his job, so I could focus on mine.

Thanks to the publishing team at Alfred A. Knopf for their patience as this project slowly developed, and then for expertly weaving it all together into a real book.

Thanks to my wife, Joan, and my sons, Evan and Joel, for making sure I had just enough time to get this done.

About the Author

DAVID ALLEN SIBLEY is the author and illustrator of the series of successful guides to nature that bear his name, including *The Sibley Guide to Birds*. He has contributed to *Smithsonian*, *Science*, *The Wilson Journal of Ornithology*, *Birding*, *BirdWatching*, and *North American Birds*, as well as to *The New York Times*. He is the recipient of the Roger Tory Peterson Award for Lifetime Achievement from the American Birding Association and the Linnaean Society of New York's Eisenmann Medal.

A Note on the Type

This book was set in Whitney Book, which belongs to a family of humanist sans-serif digital typefaces designed by American type designer Tobias Frere-Jones. It was originally created for New York's Whitney Museum as its institutional typeface. Two key requirements were flexibility for editorial requirements and a design consistency with the Whitney Museum's existing public signage.

Whitney was created in 2004 by the foundry of Hoefler & Frere-Jones. Whitney bridges the divide between editorial mainstays such as News Gothic (1908), which is an American gothic typeface, and signage application standards such as Frutiger (1975), which is a European humanist typeface.